Woandering towards places of imagination

Woandering towards places of imagination
Reflections through anarchism on the role
of educators in Early Childhood Education

Matteo Enrico Cattaneo

Södertörns högskola

Subject: Education
Research Area: Studies in the Educational Sciences
School: Teacher Education

Trycksak
3041 0865

"Welcome", Matteo Enrico Cattaneo (2022)
(image appears on pages 13 & 164)

Södertörns högskola
(Södertörn University)
The Library
SE-141 89 Huddinge
www.sh.se/publications

Cover image: "Children in Berlin", Matteo Enrico Cattaneo (2023)
Cover: Jonathan Robson
Graphic form: Per Lindblom & Jonathan Robson

Södertörn Doctoral Dissertations 230
ISSN 1652–7399

ISBN 978-91-89504-84-4 (print)
ISBN 978-91-89504-85-1 (digital)

Abstract

This dissertation proposes a reading into the transformative potential of w/o/a/ndering, anarchism and storytelling in the field of early childhood education.

Through the lenses of autoethnography, the author intertwines personal experiences with theoretical reflections, unravelling the complexities related to contemporary educational landscapes. Drawing inspiration from diverse philosophical traditions, including anarchism and existentialism, the thesis embarks on a journey to reframe educational practices within a socio-political framework.

Central to this exploration is the concept of w/o/a/ndering—a fluid interplay between wonder and wandering, symbolizing an open-ended quest for knowledge and meaning. Rooted in the works of scholars such as Luigina Mortari and Maria Zambrano, w/o/a/ndering offers a pathway to reimagine educational encounters beyond traditional pedagogical paradigms.

The thesis elucidates how storytelling emerges as a potent pedagogical tool within this framework, transcending its conventional role to become a space for encounter, play, and philosophical inquiry. By situating storytelling as a site for anarchic educational practices, the research illuminates its potential to foster genuine connections between educators and children.

Further, the dissertation examines the historical trajectory and contemporary relevance of anarchism in the educational discourse. Using the writing of theorists like Colin Ward, it explores anarchism as a lived experience, challenging entrenched power dynamics and advocating for grassroots resistance within educational settings.

In subsequent chapters, the thesis engages with the contributions of educators such as Paulo Freire, Simon Rodriguez, Walter Kohan and Janusz Korczak, emphasizing the importance of a critical pedagogy in shaping inclusive learning environments. Ultimately, this dissertation seeks to provoke critical reflection on the role of educators in shaping the present of early childhood education. By intertwining theoretical insights with practical examples, it offers a nuanced understanding of educational praxis, inviting educators to reclaim agency and foster meaningful relationships in the pursuit of holistic pedagogical objectives.

Keywords: w/o/a/ndering, anarchism, storytelling, philosophy of education, autoethnography, creative writing, critical thinking, Philosophy with Children, Early Childhood Education.

Abstract (på svenska)

Titel: W/o/a/ndering mot fantasifulla världar: Reflektioner genom anarkism om pedagogernas roll inom Early Childhood Education.

Denna avhandling föreslår en läsning av den transformativa potentialen av w/o/a/ndering, anarkism och storytelling inom området av *Early Childhood Education.*

Genom autoetnografins glasögon sammanflätar författaren personliga erfarenheter med teoretiska reflektioner och avslöjar komplexiteten i dagens pedagogiska landskap. Med inspiration från olika filosofiska traditioner, bland annat anarkism och existentialism, ger sig avhandlingen ut på en resa för att omformulera pedagogiska praktiker inom ett sociopolitiskt ramverk.

Centralt i detta utforskande är begreppet w/o/a/ndering – ett flytande samspel mellan förundran och vandring, som symboliserar ett öppet sökande efter kunskap och mening. Med rötter i arbeten av filosofer som Luigina Mortari och Maria Zambrano erbjuder w/o/a/ndering en väg att tänka nytt kring pedagogiska möten bortom traditionella pedagogiska paradigm.

Avhandlingen belyser hur storytelling framstår som ett kraftfullt pedagogiskt verktyg inom detta ramverk, som överskrider sin konventionella roll för att bli ett utrymme för möte, lek och filosofisk undersökning. Genom att placera storytelling som en plats för anarkistiska pedagogiska praxis belyser forskningen dess potential att främja äkta kontakter mellan pedagoger och barn.

Vidare undersöker avhandlingen anarkismens historiska utveckling och samtida relevans i den pedagogiska diskursen. Med hjälp av teoretiker som Colin Ward utforskas anarkism som en levd erfarenhet, som utmanar förankrad maktdynamik och förespråkar motstånd på gräsrotsnivå inom utbildningsväsendet.

I de följande kapitlen tar avhandlingen upp bidrag från pedagoger som Paulo Freire, Simon Rodríguez, Walter Kohan och Janusz Korczak, och betonar vikten av en kritisk pedagogik för att skapa inkluderande lärmiljöer. I slutändan syftar den här avhandlingen till att väcka kritisk reflektion kring pedagogernas roll i utformningen av dagens förskoleverksamhet. Genom att varva teoretiska insikter med praktiska exempel ger avhandlingen en nyanserad förståelse av pedagogisk praxis, och uppmanar pedagoger att återta sitt handlingsutrymme och skapa meningsfulla relationer i strävan efter att uppnå holistiska pedagogiska mål.

Nyckelord: w/o/a/ndering, anarkism, storytelling, utbildningsfilosofi, autoetnografi, kreativt skrivande, kritiskt tänkande, filosofi med barn, förskolepedagogik.

Acknowledgments

It is strange to have come this far. If I think to my teenage years, well, then it is even overwhelming. First and foremost, I want to thank my wife Pauline, that has been my precious light through this w/o/a/ndering. She has been there every step, and I can well say that I couldn't make it without her endless support. My children too, Emma and Enea, all the hugs and kisses I got from them were really important. Moreover, they helped me think more and more about the relationship that we adult can create with children, and which possibilities childhood can offer in our w/o/a/ndering.

Then I would like to thank Niclas Månsson, my main supervisor, as his openness, insights, pep-talk when it was difficult, have been really appreciated. Moreover, thanks to him I have learned what to do to be a good supervisor. A thank to Viktor Johansson, my co-supervisor for his insights, and enriching talks about pedagogy and philosophy. Love and gratitude to Walter Kohan who has encouraged me to pursue a Ph.D., and to be a such an inspiration.

Then I would like to thank my colleagues at Södertörn University Emma, Lotta, Shelby and Carolina, unfortunately Covid didn't help our time at SH but happy to have had you as colleagues. Especially Maša, for the endless talks, encouragements, and insights, I think we have supported each other well through this time. Thank you Kristina, to have shared with me passions and warm conversations. A special thanks to Liza Haglund for her support behind the scenes in these years. I would also like to thank Kim Silow Kallenberg, for her insights and encouragement towards a more creative writing and Eva Schwarz. And of course, Jan-Erik Mansikka your comments and your positivity have been really appreciated and needed. A special thanks to Joanna Haynes who gladly accepted to be the opponent to my dissertation. Moreover, I would like to mention Lorenzo Molfese for the discussions we had during the proof reading of this dissertation. I would also like to thank all my new colleagues at Gävle University, you have welcomed me in the best possible way.

A special thanks to my parents that in a way or another have been there, much before this dissertation. Thank you to my brothers and sister and the whole family. A special thanks to Barbara for our walks and talks. A warm appreciation to Roberto for his friendship and inspiration. Finally, thank you to my lifelong friends Pascal, Daniele, Monica, Don Patrizio, Stefano. A thanks to Katia to have introduced me to philosophy. Everyone has contributed in different ways to this w/o/a/ndering started years ago. With this thesis I'd like to remember my grandparents, they would probably be proud of this w/o/a/ndering, and moreover Professor Fulvio Manara.

*Alle mie due stelle, Emma ed Enea.
Illuminate il cammino verso luoghi di immaginazione,
continuate a guardare il mondo con occhi diversi e bontà.
Con amore.*

Contents

If one is truly to succeed in leading a person to a specific place,
one must first and foremost take care to find him where he is
and begin there.
Søren Kierkegaard

If you take care of the small things,
the big things take care of themselves.
You can gain more control over your life
by paying closer attention to the little things.
Emily Dickinson

CHAPTER ONE

Overture

I look at my bookshelves. The afternoon sun paints the living room orange. Among the shelves there is no logical 'order' in the placement of books. Novels, philosophical treatises, books on politics, education, figure books, photography books and others are next to each other. I like to think that the only common thread between them is that they are stories, no matter what stories. Among them, I can also spot some journals I have written over the years. One of them takes me back to a time in my life, a fleeting instant of time happened years ago.

I was finishing my second year of studies in literature and philosophy and, in the meantime, I was working as a scenographer for a theatre collective. Studying literature and philosophy was a choice I made due to an interest developed in high school. Whereas being a scenographer was a totally unexpected path. Little did I know, however, that there was a new adventure just around the corner.

An adventure that came in the form of a letter, from the army. I had been called up for conscription. WHAT!? I really didn't expect it. My job as a scenographer took me around Italy, my status as a student occupied my remaining time, and so that year I forgot to apply for deferment. I had no choice but to report to the army station just after the summer. Meanwhile, I kept thinking about how I could avoid military duty. In Italy, at the time, you could object to conscription and do community service instead.

This marks the beginning of my journey as an educator. During my high school years, I engaged in voluntary work within my parish community. Throughout the school year, I assisted children with their homework and participated in their recreational activities. Additionally, during summer breaks, when I wasn't working as a carpenter, I dedicated time to community service within my parish. This experience was both rewarding and challenging. It was within this familiar setting that I had the opportunity to develop a closer relationship with don Patrizio, the parish priest who cared for the children and youth. Twenty-five years have passed since my initial involvement in that community, yet the bond with him remains deeply ingrained within me. From don Patrizio I learned a form of radical humanism.

However, it was something that happened a couple of years after this experience that changed my educational perspective. When my work for the parish was concluded, I began working in different educational contexts in early childhood. In one of these contexts, I met an educator, or rather a psychomotor therapist. I knew what psychomotor education was, but I had never thought it could be a professional alternative for me. So, I decided to enrol on a course, but I needed an internship and got in touch with a centre in my city.

The psychomotor sessions took place in a room, there were 2–3 educators and about ten children. In this room there was a world inviolable from the outside. A room that resembled the world at the end of the tunnel, just like the rabbit hole in Lewis Carroll's story: a world full of wonder. Whatever happened in the room remained within its walls. This ensured that the children could express themselves freely, free from the fear of being judged. The rules, apart from those regarding physical safety, were arranged between the children and the educators. In this room, play was truly free as we educators were 'only' facilitators. Yet we were also an integral part of the children's play and storytelling. Psychomotricity aims at the development of the child in a holistic way, that means that children have the possibility to grow according to his or her subjectivity in relation to the circumstances.

As I said, anything that happened and was said in the room remained in the room. If children had the wish to share with their parents what happened inside the room they could, and in case we needed to speak with parents about a specific event that occurred in the room we could talk only after the children's permission. A room meant to be a sort of sanctuary, a place of freedom and equality. However, besides the therapeutical side, what I found truly fascinating was the ability children had to make their own world, to make their own rules, and to create a small society based on freedom, equality, and cooperation through stories. This experience opened my eyes to a different approach towards children. I must say that I kept several aspects of it as tools in my practice as an educator in Early Childhood Education (ECE). It helped me think about education, about the relationship that we have with children in a completely different way. There, I began to question my role as an adult, as an educator.

Why tell this episode?

This dissertation is based on my experience as an educator in preschools and early childhood education centers, and I wanted to narrate how the sparkle of my interest in stories, pedagogical philosophy and anarchism ignited. As a student at the university and as an educator in early childhood education, I have always been fascinated by authors who clearly showed their ideas about education in relation to their lives and who are close to the idea of *praxis*[1] proposed by the Brazilian philosopher and educator Paulo Freire. The educators, philosophers and scholars that will be presented in this dissertation have been following me for many years. Their books are well visible on my bookshelf as a daily reminder. If I enjoyed being an educator, a part of some pedagogical and educational space, and a doctoral student in education, it is thanks to their works and praxis. There, I found meaning in my own work. In this dissertation I will use the concept of w/o/a/ndering[2]. A concept that will be helpful in order to read these authors and understand their philosophy and pedagogy portrayed in this thesis. At the same time, this is a concept that we could use as educators in our practices.

During my years as a student in pedagogy, I had the opportunity to create my own curriculum, trying to include courses in anthropology, philosophy, sociology and, of course, pedagogy. My aim was to delve into the human being in its holistic nature. Attending a course of philosophy of education, I once met a professor, Fulvio Manara, and thanks to him I began reading authors such as Paulo Freire, Walter Kohan, Maria Zambrano, Luigina Mortari, and many others. Authors who helped me reflect on the educator-educatee relationship, and authors who questioned the position of educators in educational practice. Moreover, through Manara, I got in touch with the practice of Philosophy for Children and Community of Inquiry[3], a practice that was grounded by Matthew Lipman and Margareth Sharp.[4] An educational praxis that allowed me to mix storytelling and philosophy and that I have tried to enhance through playtime. An educational practice that I believe could also foster anarchist principles.

Professor Manara encouraged me to keep on studying after my bachelor's degree, so I got a master's degree where he was my supervisor… and then he encouraged me to pursue a Ph.D. Probably this encounter is the second "episode" that brought me here, not only as a doctoral student but as an educator. Using a figure of speech, he used to say that we had to take care of our candle because if we can protect the light of the candle, then we can see the surroundings, which means the others. I always keep his words within me, they are like a compass that helps the wanderer find his way. As an early childhood educator, I have to observe the road every day and make the road with whoever walks it with me.

Therefore, I would like to propose a reflection capable of framing early childhood education practice not as something immutable but as a space where, despite structural difficulties, we educators can find the possibility of practicing with a gentle time. By gentle time, I mean a time in which children and educators can meet without thinking about a final product to show, without being judged as a physical product. But, instead, a time where everyone can take "their" time to experience themselves.

The problem and the purpose of this work

This thesis serves as both a pedagogical and philosophical reflection, weaving the experiences and reflections of various educators. These narratives intersect with my own practice and reflections.

The purpose of this dissertation is to explore the concept of w/o/a/ndering in order to enrich the idea of anarchist practice in early childhood education, so that educators can adopt creative transformative learning practices. Furthermore, I believe storytelling can be seen as a space that embodies both practices.

Specifically, the concept of w/o/a/ndering is distilled from the educational and theoretical experiences of authors such as Maria Zambrano, Luigina Mortari and Walter Kohan. Moreover, it is important to underline that this dissertation should be read through this concept. This means that I relate and understand anarchism and autoethnography, as well as scholars and philosophers displayed in these pages, through the work of Mortari and subsequently Zambrano. Furthermore, the concept of anarchism, being a broad philosophical and political movement, both in time and content, which has evolved and continues to evolve, will be identified in the practice and theory of Colin Ward and through his idea of daily anarchism. Finally, the practice of storytelling will be understood in a broad perspective, not only stories told or heard, but also play as a potential philosophical practice. Storytelling then is understood as a fostering space where w/o/a/ndering and anarchism can emerge. In addition, the dissertation itself should be read as a storytelling practice. As an autoethnographer, I intend to reflect on how our role as educators could foster imaginative thinking, cultural awareness, a sense of self and community, and also a sense of belonging. In this dissertation, personal narratives and stories serve as vehicles for self-discovery and transformation, leading through an interdisciplinary framework to a more profound understanding of the educator's role.[5] The reflections that I will engage with in this dissertation cannot be answered in definitive and absolute terms. It is an ever-evolving criticism.

It is then important to read these pages with the idea of *in the spirit of.* I took this recontextualizing approach from a reflection that Freire used to make about his pedagogy, which had to be reinvented, and this is what I am proposing here: an attempt to reinvent or rethink some pedagogies.[6] I also believe that it is important to consider educators as bricoleurs or agents who, given a space, a task and a time, can invent a way of being and doing. This reminds me of what Pacini-Ketchabaw says about the complexity of the work of educators.[7] For this reason, the artisan craft of educating is difficult.

A critical reflection emerges here, we must acknowledge that much of the discourse about children is authored by adults and this echoes the sentiment expressed by Malaguzzi and Lorenzoni according to whom we often talk about children but fail to truly listen to them.[8] Educators are under enormous pressure from the "outside" world, parents and society, in order to perform and give measurable results. Schools, according to a neo-liberal model, have been incorporated into the market, and parents and children are clients. This way, the educational relationship fades, and it is harder to have a child-educator relationship, consequently their relationship becomes vertical rather than horizontal.[9] These reflections also emerged in the classroom at the university where I teach, where students are concerned about their future role as educators in early childhood education. The school system in the liberal-democratic world intends the school as a place which produces the human being of tomorrow, conceived as a piece of a bigger puzzle.[10] That is why the revitalization of the idea of anarchism within education is an important development embedded in this dissertation. When thinking of anarchism Colin Ward and Tomás Ibanez underline how important it is to think of it as a moment, an action to be accompanied in daily life. By this, they mean that it is impossible to completely change society, especially in a single revolutionary action, but by intertwining anarchist's scratches with moment of everyday life, it is possible to integrate an anarchist praxis into current thought.

Investigating Klaus Mollenhauer's *Forgotten Connection,* Friesen and Sævi ask these questions: "What way of life do I present to children by living with them? What way of life ought to be systematically represented to children? How can I help children to become self-starters and support their growth? Who am I? Who do I want to be, and how do I help others with their identity?"[11] As an educator I ask myself these questions, questions that could be even found in anarchism and in the existentialist philosophy of Mortari and Zambrano. I believe it is important, in our role as educators, to think about what is happening in the world around us. If we want to change the path taken by society, we need to be the first example for the children. This is where the importance of the preschool comes in, since in preschool the most important things are attention and care. Lorenzoni cherished observing the spontaneous play of children, their ability to transform their surroundings and create imaginary worlds based on their experiences. He argues that children, inherently utopian by nature, haven't got so much space since adults do not seem very keen on making room for them.[12] While this thesis has the intention of enriching the thought on the role of the educator, it also affirms the enormous educational possibilities that preschools have, where children are given not only the opportunity to learn but to be. Together, children and adults, can foster and develop their own experience and awareness. To be aware means also listening and observing carefully to the other, it means to be attentive, as Ingold suggests.[13] Through w/o/a/ndering we can attune to children and foster a sense of belonging. Through w/o/a/ndering we can imagine and enhance a pedagogical praxis that attunes to the circumstances we are in.

Storytelling as a daily anarchist possibility

Inside an early childhood education center, there are different moments, or activities, both during the day and during the week. For this reason, I decided to identify as an anarchist pocket a typical human practice, which is storytelling.[14] We can all, albeit in different ways, tell or listen to stories. Through stories, we can share our human culture and we can relate to others. Storytelling can transform itself, it has a malleability that helps educators and children build a common space that is shared as equals, a gentle space as I call it. Of course, it could be used for the wrong purpose, creating a negative narration that could mislead. We could think of the narrative that dictatorships create, or in a more educational contexts the narration "against" other classmates can create events of bullying. That is why it is important for educators to use storytelling to be aware not only of the positive but also the negative potential. This way we can try to make this practice critical with children.

I use the term storytelling, a term that is widely used but sometimes misinterpreted or abused. In Latin *narration* is not only telling, but also gathering.[15] So, I understand storytelling as the possibility of telling stories, but also of collecting them, of asking questions, of reflecting, and intrinsically it is a possibility of dialogue, between the one who sows and the one who harvests. Through storytelling we can create an educational practice with a shared horizon.

It is not easy to place my work in a field, especially when the literature on it is not extensive. I mean that the field of early childhood education has not often crossed path with anarchism. Judith Suissa underlines how anarchism in its theoretical formulation has given little space to the analysis of educational practices.[16] I am not stating that there have not been and there are no anarchist educational practices, but they are sporadic. For example, in Spain between the end of the 19th and the beginning of the 20th century, the Catalan educator and anarchist Francisco Ferrer y Guardia founded a school known as *La Escuela Moderna*.[17] A school that was closed after his death. Ferrer was executed for being an anarchist, as he was an inconvenience to the Church and the State. Subsequently other schools based on Ferrer Y Guardia's idea were opened in the United States. Some of those which are very close, overlapping or overtly anarchist examples are the Sundbury Valley School, the Celestin Freinet's school, the Movimento di Cooperazione Educativa,[18] or the schools connected to EUDEC's network. Anyway, it is for this reason that Ward's concept of daily anarchism is useful, as anarchism can be practiced in fleeting pockets. Ward says that these pockets are micro-revolutions, and anarchism must be seen as a micro-revolution.[19] What I am suggesting here is that we can think of stories the same way Ward thought about anarchism, that is to say that stories can be defined as anarchist pockets.

This suggestion comes from the reading of the concept of micro-politics proposed by Kelchtermans and Ballet.[20] They suggest that teachers have normative ideas about good teaching and how they are to be achieved in practice. The article underlined that each school as an organization has traditions and habits, together with subtle power relations between school members, and each of these actors have different interests. This is but a sip of micro-politics and as Keltchtermans and Ballet said quoting the observation of Schempp, "the classroom responsibilities facing the inductees had less to do with teaching children and more to do with juggling the multiple demands of a functioning institution".[21] It is proper to say that the concept of micropolitics has to be seen as the strategies and tactics used by individuals and groups in an organization to encourage their interests.[22] Moreover, as Kelchtermans and Ballet explained, micropolitical processes simply occurs in any organization, in the process of collaboration as well as in resistance, and within the organization as well as in the interactions with the external environment.[23] Hence, the examination of educational practices emphasizes the personal or collective understands of political processes by organization members. This encompasses their choices, values, interests, motives, and individual career narratives interwoven with the school's history.[24]

In my understanding of storytelling, I see the opportunity to have a praxis that could adapt itself to the circumstances, stretching and extending like a bubble gum, a helpful quality to enhance the curriculum. When I said that anarchism could potentially be found everywhere, I mean that many scholars, even if they don't officially belong to an anarchist movement, can however foster some anarchical thought and understanding. However, it is also important to underline that the storytelling moment we have at school is not the only thing we could consider as an anarchist pocket, but the dissertation itself can be considered as such.

Conclusion

My intention through this introduction was to give an overview of some insights regarding the role of the educator, anarchism, storytelling and stories, as well as early childhood education studies. I have used the concept of micropolitics in relation to storytelling in an effort to connect this practice to the idea of anarchism. The practice of storytelling can also be seen as a piece of clay that can be modelled according to needs and context. With this interpretation of plasticity, it becomes possible to appreciate the idea of an educator who, depending on the circumstances in which s/he finds her-himself, has the possibility of shaping an activity, in this case, storytelling, in order to obtain, or at least try to obtain, a meaningful educational practice for the educator and educatees. To have a meaningful educational practice it is important to create a relationship of mutual trust as anarchism preaches. My intention is to relate several ideas, concepts, and approaches within education, to storytelling's practice, which is to be intended as a micropolitical space where educators and educatees have the possibility to experiment themselves to foster a meaningful educational practice.

Thesis Disposition

This thesis has been developed in an unexpected way, probably like many other dissertations. At the beginning, I had planned to develop my dissertation within a *formal* framework: an introduction, then chapters about method, theory, empiric material, analysis, and discussion. However the more time passed, the more and more influences moulded my understanding. In this sense, authors like Ingold, Lorenzoni and Kohan *encouraged me* to think differently in the composition of an academic text. Moreover, I discovered the practice of autoethnography that gave me the possibility to write more freely. This thesis has eight chapters, which are connected to each other, but they are also autonomous in a certain way. The red thread between the chapters is the concept of anarchism and the concept of w/o/a/ndering. It is then correct to assume that this dissertation has to be read through the insights that Mortari and Zambrano offered us.

The first chapter has pointed out what I am seeking in this thesis and the field where it is situated, that is early childhood education, and how it would contribute to the educational field. The second chapter is about the method used to approach this work, which is inspired by autoethnography. I argue that this dissertation could be read as a book experience, and that it is important to read other experiences in order to better understand your own. In the third chapter I display the work of the Italian scholar Luigina Mortari and the Spanish philosopher Maria Zambrano. In particular, I will focus on the reading of Zambrano that Mortari does and I will emphasize the idea of w/o/a/ndering and how I used and use it as an educator in Early Childhood Education. The fourth chapter addresses the theme of storytelling, and it fosters a philosophical and pedagogical reflection on it. Moreover, I will display how narrating stories is an innate peculiarity of the human being and how they help us contextualize ourselves within the society we belong to. The fifth chapter gives an overview of anarchism and some main concepts are briefly displayed. Then through the work of the British anarchist Colin Ward, I intend to display a more practical vision of anarchism and education. I have tried to connect and reflect on educational practices like storytelling, and more in general, on the role of educators in their daily practice with children. The sixth chapter develops reflections on education, through the work and lives of educators like Jacques Rancière, Joseph Jacotot, Simòn Rodrìguez, Walter Kohan and Janusz Korczak. All of them contributed to redefine the idea of a philosophical life through their pedagogical practice and reflection, and I believe that all of them, in a way, have developed an autoethnographic methodology, and even though not overtly anarchists, they have still lived or live a daily anarchism as imagined by Ward. The seventh chapter is about Paulo Freire's work, and I delve into some of his concepts and relate them to the educational practice in Early Childhood Education.

Finally in the eighth and last chapter I will sum up the work done, what perspectives there may be and how to develop the points discussed in the dissertation.

A last note, in some part of the dissertation the font will be *different*, and in those section my personal position, my autoethnographical voice will be displayed, just like I did in the introduction to this chapter.

Notes

[1] Paulo Freire introduced it in his first work *Pedagogy of Oppressed* (2000). According to Freire praxis is understood as *action* and *reflection* together create this equation *word=work=praxis*. Freire argues that authentic education is not carried on by **a** *for* **b** or by **a** *about* **b** but rather **a** *with* **b**. This happens through praxis.

[2] It will be displayed in the next chapter.

[3] www.icpic.org; www.sapere.org.uk; https://junior.filosofia.unimi.it/corsi-di-filosofia-per-bambini-in-italia/

[4] Pritchard, Michael, "Philosophy for Children", *The Stanford Encyclopedia of Philosophy*, (Summer 2022 Edition), Edward N. Zalta (ed.), URL=<https://plato.stanford.edu/archives/sum2022/entries/children/>

[5] Mortari, Luigina. *Cultura della ricerca pedagogica.* (Roma: Carocci, 2007).

[6] Freie, 2014b. "One day at the beginning of my travels around the world, I was asked, I don't remember where, "Paulo, what can we do in order to follow you?" And I said, if you follow me, you destroy me. The best way to understand me is to reinvent me and not to try to become adapted to me. Experience cannot be exported, it can only be reinvented".

[7] Pacini-Ketchabaw, Veronica et al. *Journeys, Reconceptualizing ECP through Pedagogical narration.* Toronto: UTP, 2015.

[8] Malaguzzi 2016; Lorenzoni 2023.

[9] (Codello 2105, Rinaldi 2009, Malaguzzi 2016, Maschelein and Simmons 2006, 2008, 2013; Biesta 2015, 2017, 2021; Eriksson, 2020; Kohan 2004, 2014, 2021, 2022; Ward 1995, 2014; Chomsky 2004; Lodi, 2022; Lorenzoni 2014, 2019, 2023; Goodman 1971, 2012).

[10] (Codello 2105, Rinaldi 2009, Malaguzzi 2016, Maschelein and Simmons 2006, 2008, 2013; Biesta 2015, 2017, 2021; Eriksson, 2020; Kohan 2004, 2014, 2021, 2022; Ward 1995, 2014; Chomsky 2004; Lodi, 2022; Lorenzoni 2014, 2019, 2023; Goodman 1971, 2012).

[11] Tone Sævi and Norm Friesen (2010) 'Reviving forgotten connections in North American teacher education: Klaus Mollenhauer and the pedagogical relation', Journal of Curriculum Studies, 42, pp. 123–147.

[12] Lorenzoni, Franco. *Educare controvento.* (Palermo: Sellerio, 2023).

[13] Ingold 2018.

[14] Gottschall, Jonathan. *The storytelling animals.* (New York: Mariner, 2013); Bruner, Jerome. *Making Stories.* (Harvard: Harvard University Press, 2003); Bruner, Jerome. *La ricerca del significato: per una psicologia culturale.* (Torino: Bollati Boringhieri, 1992)

[15] Castiglioni, Luigi. *Dizionario della lingua latina.* (Milano: Loescher, 2019).

[16] Suissa, Judith. *Anarchism and education: a philosophical perspective.* (Oakland: PM press, 2010).

[17] Haworth, Robert H. *Anarchist education and the Modern School.* (Oakland: PM Press, 2019) For example it is worth to mention other schools or practices like, Sundbury Valley school, Celestine Freinet's school, or in modern days the school connected to the network EUDEC.

[18] Trasatti, Filippo. *Lessico Minimo di Pedagogia Libertaria.* (Milano: Eleuthèra Editrice, 2014).

[19] Ward, Colin. *Anarchy in Action.* (Oakland: PM Press, 2018).

[20] Kelchtermans, Geert and Ballet, Katrjin. The Micropolitics of Teacher Induction: A Narrative-Biographical Study on Teacher Socialization. *Teaching and Teacher Education*, 18, 2002. 105–120.

[21] Schempp, Paul. The Micro-politics of Teacher Induction. *American Educational Research Journal*, 30 (3), 1993 pp. 447–472. p.459.

[22] Kelchtermans and Ballet 2002, p.105.

[23] Kelchtermans and Ballet 2002, p.108.

[24] Kelchtermans and Ballet 2002.

I have come to ask myself:
if reality is different for each person,
is it possible to speak of a singular reality or
should we perhaps speak of a plurality of realities instead?
And if there is a plurality of realities,
are there more true (or real) than others?
Philip K. Dick

The attentive eye makes the world interesting.
Rebecca Norris-Webb

Life can only be understood backwards; but it must be lived forwards.
Søren Kierkegaard

CHAPTER TWO

Approaching autoethnography

In this chapter I will display the method of autoethnography used to carry out the research of this thesis. Autoethnography has played an important role in developing the understanding of my practice and writing, and here I would like to relate it to Walter Kohan's idea of *book-experience.*

Since I also understand the autoethnographic method through the concept of w/o/a/ndering, this same concept will be shown at the beginning of this chapter and examined in more depth in the following one. The idea of w/o/a/ndering is grounded and reconceptualized from the work of Italian scholar and philosopher Luigina Mortari's *Un metodo a-metodico,* where she reframes the work of the Spanish philosopher Maria Zambrano.[25] Being the word a gerundive[26], it gives us the idea of something in *becoming.* Thus, Mortari proposes a philosophical-pedagogical method that helps to be critical towards our pedagogical practice.

In developing the concept of w/o/a/ndering, the influence of Walter Kohan's books, *El Maestro Inventor*[27] and *Viajar para vivir: ensayar*[28] as well as Mortari's *Un Metodo a-Metodico,* have been important.[29] I also mention the pedagogical work of the Italian teacher Carla Melanzini who brought outside school's wall educational practices in one of the most problematic neighbourhood in Naples in order to give to every child a possibility to have a proper education, and we can appreciate her work in the book *Insegnare al Principe di Danimarca.*[30] In the book *El Maestro Inventor,* Kohan portrays the life of the educator and the philosopher Simòn Rodrìguez, and through Rodrìguez's life he reflects on the role of educators in our society. Kohan does a profound description of Rodrìguez's attitude to life, discovery, philosophy, and the idea of wonder and wander are both being used. The same theme could be read in the work of Mortari, where through the words of Zambrano, she displays the possibility to unveil the world around us in an evolving awareness. Thanks to these scholars we can understand, as educators in early childhood education, that our educational practice is an opening of doors towards possibilities. The practice of storytelling for example can help educators create such possibilities. As human beings we can tell and read stories, we can wonder, and we can wander through them.

W/o/a/ndering: a first approach

I have always found English words fascinating, especially when they are so close in their sound and sometimes in their deeper meaning, just like *w/a/ndering* and *w/o/ndering*. The first word is a verb and indicates when someone walks or moves leisurely or aimlessly. The second verb indicates when someone has a feeling of amazement and admiration, caused by something beautiful, remarkable, or unfamiliar, and it means the desire to know something and feel curious but also doubtful about it. These two concepts are important to me on so many different levels: they are essential in my understanding, in my practice as an educator in early childhood education, as a father, a researcher and activist. Freire himself suggests the importance of wandering in the world to be inspired.[31] This approach to education intertwines biography, pedagogy, and philosophy.

Kohan states that it is important to meet others and "understand oneself through others, to be exposed to differences and diversity".[32] For this reason I perceive the idea of education as an act of craftsmanship where the educator learns to make and remake his or her practice, in a continuous becoming, as Mortari has suggested.[33] In other words, it is through the encounter with the other, with diversity, that I am able to understand myself. In this way, making a mistake becomes important too, since it is through mistakes that we can learn and improve, given that we look at them in a self-critical attitude. Furthermore, in his drawing of wandering, Kohan portrays Freire's errancy of ideas. Kohan defines Freire as a connective boy, since in his philosophical and educational journey he has always tried to connect different ideas, sometimes where there are no apparent ties.[34] This is also what I try to do in my approach to education and research: I look for possibilities. If we embrace this approach as educators we can try to find new relations, we can create new reflections, reframe our actions, and then foster new praxis.[35]

I have already mentioned that w/o/a/ndering is a gerund, a verbal adjective. In *Historia como Sistema* Ortega y Gasset said: that the grammatical form of human life is the gerundive because it is ever-changing, it is a *facendum*, not a *factum*.[36] Life is not something definitive and given, but it goes on, and something always happens in life. It is something given to us, but we must build it ourselves.[37] What interests me in Ortega y Gasset's concept is the fact that life is an act in progress, it is not static, and therefore with this premise, the concept of w/o/a/ndering takes on even more meaning.[38] Overall we should think at awareness as an evolving process.

In his book *The Life of Lines* the anthropologist and scholar Tim Ingold suggests that the human being should be seen as a line, which follows its own way, changing direction, twisting and still going. A line that intersects with other lines, which can be seen as other lives and other bios. The lines, therefore, the bios, are not entities enclosed as bubbles can be, which remain "isolated" from other bubbles[39]. A typical feature of these lines, thus, is that they are in perpetual motion, intertwining with other lines. "The rope is always weaving, always in process and-like social life itself- never finished"[40] Ingold argues that the lines are free, it is true that they intertwine with other lines, but the point is that they are free to move and intertwine. However, I find the conclusions of Ingold's book quite interesting as he states:

> ... anthropology has the means and the determination to show how knowledge grows from the crucible of lives lived with others, in the in-between. This knowledge consists not in propositions about the world but in the skills of perception and capacities of judgement that develop in the course of direct, practical and sensuous engagements with the beings and things with whom, and with which, we share our lives.[41]

I see Ingold's statement as a suggestion to the understanding of w/o/a/ndering and educational anarchism. Both concepts engage with an existential ontology and a practice of relationship with the world that surrounds us. I mean an ontology that arise from existential experience, life questions. In this way I relate it to a world made of people and things. A world made by stories. A world, in which we are a part of, always in becoming, where individuality, not individualism, should be encouraged. An individuality that finds its confirmation in the relationship with the other.

Referring to the different kinds of Philosophy for Children, Walter Kohan once said that there are no good or bad practices, but each one can contribute to transform reality, we just have to choose which one suits us more since each choice is political.[42] This argument suggests that when we pick up a method, we propose a vision or a perspective of the world, we are offering our own contribution to the field, and so there is also a political dimension in our praxis.

The approaches of autoethnography as well as of w/o/a/ndering are not trying to give general rules but they try to reflect on a single phenomenon. Autoethnography provides us with an interpretation-based approach, where we as researchers need to interpret the contextual reality and try to understand relationships, subjects, objects, and the world.

In quest of a voice

I have a rather broad interest in reading preferences, however the stories where the human being is questioned, where there is a sense of w/o/a/ndering, are the ones that I find the most engaging. For example, in McCarthy's book *The Road*, a child with his father is walking in a post-apocalyptic world, everything is destroyed and society has no rules. The son asks his father for reassurance. The father responds that "nothing bad is going to happen to us. Because we're carrying the fire".[43] The fire represents hope, it is the will to live nobly, and make moral and ethical decisions. In truth, we don't live in a post-apocalyptic world, but as a father and educator in early childhood education, I questioned myself whether I was carrying the fire or not. How can I carry and share the fire with others? This is the meaning of w/o/a/ndering, both for me and for the characters in McCarthy's novel.

The scholars and philosophers I mention in this dissertation are not only pedagogical and philosophical examples but important references for my way of writing too. A way of writing that, as defined and reiterated by Freire, recalls the oral tradition.[44] A voice close to the reader. This is due to the oral status of Freire written word, where the relevance of a theme is maintained by speaking about an array of different topics keeping always a curious approach.[45]

Another important step in my process of writing and composing a text comes from what Wozniak said about Kohan's books, *The Inventive School-master* or *Paulo Freire, a Philosophical Biography*, as they both have an approach that could be defined as *philosophical pedagogical-biography* (biografía filosófico-educacional). That is to say that:

> philosophical pedagogical-biography can create book experiences which are at once disruptive, in that they interrupt our habitual ways of thinking about philosophy, life, and education, while also being formative, in that they inspire us to cultivate alternative manners of philosophizing, living, and educating.[46]

I don't know if I will get close to what Kohan succeeds in doing, but the road I want to walk on has already been traced. Kohan tries to decolonize childhood, and his insights overlap with Ward's vision about childhood and adulthood[47]. This is what I would like to propose with my writing.

To achieve this, one should employ a writing style that keeps some distance from the traditional way of composing a text according to the academic standard. I think that a more creative way of writing and doing research could benefit the academic world, overall. It could show many different shades. In this regard, I have discovered different forms of doctoral theses, and this pushed me to keep the direction of my writing and so the hope is to keep this poetic sound in my own writing. It is interesting to notice what Zambrano suggests in *Note di un Metodo,* as she argues that, when writing, the writer should think to a melody rather than a rhythm. According to Zambrano the melody is something in becoming, a transformative experience, while the rhythm is something structured, immutable. In this understanding, as researchers, scholars, and educators, we might want to consider a writing style that resembles a melody more than a rhythm.[48]

Leafing through the pages of Walter Kohan's *Childhood, Education and Philosophy*[49] I found an interesting invitation as a writer: to write under a different, a logic which is based on experience. If one writes with his or her own educational experience in mind, it can open the door to the reader for a different kind of experience, where the truth is no longer transmitted but, as Kohan points out, it is "rather to put our relationship to them into question"[50] and then he continues:

> I do so in a world, the academic one, that as we were saying has distanced itself from life, it has built its own world, its own rules, its own life. Sometimes shaded, subdued, evasive, giving its back to the world of life, in the middle of that world we live.[51]

This questioning and vision gave me the opportunity to look at my own practice, my ideas, and my reflections with new eyes. Maybe it is correct to say I feel less lonely since I share the same idea with someone else. In his lines, there is a spirit that is possible to relate to what, a few pages before, I have introduced as w/o/a/ndering or also to the anarchist approach to education, as both try to investigate life and the daily experience.

The aim here is to underline how to read this dissertation, which is an attempt to provide a book-experience. The experiences that serve as a ground for this dissertation are the ones of several educators and scholars, combined with mine. A common ground that will help us reflect upon the role and mostly the relationship that educators have towards children. Moreover, it is also through other hi/stories, or circumstances, that we, as educators, might have the possibility to give meaning to our profession.[52] A book based on experience could then enhance a collective narration. The practice of the educators and philosophers that are displayed in this thesis should be understood as a point of departure, not a point of arrival. Their and my experiences cannot be translated in every single context but should be critically reinvented.

Elizabeth Henderson, in her book *Autoethnography in Early Childhood Education and Care,* shares both mine and Kohan's concern about the distance of academia from the world.[53] A distance which aims to produce a truth to be read tout court, where personal experience is not always welcomed. This is the reason why I turn my gaze to autoethnography.

Henderson argues that during the writing of her essay, she experienced discomfort, she didn't know how to share her stories, her emotions, and her reflections.[54] She felt as if she did not fit into the academia and couldn't find a connection to most of the paradigms and methodologies.[55] At the end of her journey, she came to the conclusion that she didn't want to lose her voice and her stories, and so the road to autoethnography was finally open.

However, in facing this quest for a voice, I believe it is worth mentioning the idea of *circunstancia* that Josè Ortega y Gasset offers in Meditaciones del Quixote. In this seminal work, Ortega y Gasset writes: *"yo soy yo y mi circunstancia y su no la salvo a ella no me salvo yo"*[56] (I am I and my circumstances and if I don't save it I don't save myself either). Ortega means we are who we are, and that the circumstances we were and are in will always mould us. It is important to remember from where we come from as *ubi consistam* (as a stable ground) in order to take new roads and not to be afraid to lose ourselves in our w/o/a/ndering. Ortega y Gasset means that we as human beings are unique, and we can't transfer to another human being what we are. In other words, nobody can live for me, or I can't live for others as well. Our uniqueness is defined by the time (historical) and space that we live in, this means it is impossible to divide the biography with the thoughts and actions we generate, thoughts born after our experiences which are unique.

From my perspective, I understand human beings as *biologos.* With biologos I mean the ontological and epistemological condition of the human being which is impossible to separate from the being itself. In Greek the word *bio* means life while *logos* means to tell, to think, but the root of logos is *leghein* which means to preserve or collect, in other words to welcome what it is said and therefore to listen. It is within this interpretation and understanding of the word's *bio* and *logos* that I propose and understand the concept of *bio-logos.* My definition of *bio-logos* is the movement that a human being does (or should do) daily where, in the act of *bio (living)* through *logos (the ability to tell, think, listen, preserve),* he welcomes the other and presents the self to the other. Through this movement, the being has its *raison d'être.* I understand this *bio-logos* as an ontological and epistemological dimension.

We are what we are through our actions, our *logos* is the epistemological dimension, while our *bio* is the ontological one.

Biologos denotes our *constitutiveness* as *narrating beings,* in other words, each of us is moulded by our *circumstances.* Through personal storytelling, individuals share their world with others, finding meaning within their own experiences and collaboratively crafting new narratives, worlds, and circumstances together.

It is to this extent that I understand the potential within a philosophical narration. I can see the possibility to develop not only the concepts of education and childhood but to enhance or reflect upon the concept of *collective biography*, a concept that helps to go beyond and connect time and space.[57] My understanding of collective biography is that the biographies that are told and lived by someone create a collective memory, and this memory transcends time and space. For instance, this dissertation could be seen as collective biography, where my praxis is grounded on others' book-experience, and this builds up a collective reflection. We can think of it as a house made of bricks, each brick is a biography, educators or educatees, and together we build a house. Layer after layer. Mollenhauer suggests that:

> education's purpose is to further the cause of memory. By memory I mean collective memory-our common cultural heritage whose core themes education attempts to tease out: its principles, viewpoints and norms around which memory can orient itself. (...) Education should focus on cultural and biographical memory, and should seek lasting principles in this memory that develop the child's potential.[58]

This idea of collective biography could be related to anarchism as well. I understand anarchism as the expression of an individuality within a group. My experience intertwines with others' experiences, like the stories we tell and we collect. Within an anarchist setting our collaboration becomes a collective learning experience, where we can learn from each other. With the word learning I don't mean merely knowledge, I mean a way to stay together, to collaborate, to share, to listen, to observe, to speak up. To rethink my own position in relation to the circumstancia.

Autoethnography: an understanding

Autoethnography has been a recent discovery in my academic life. When I began as a doctoral student, I planned to do empirical research, but due to several circumstances I changed my path. I did not know about autoethnography, I had heard about it, but not so much more. Then I attended a course in Creative Academic Writing to try to improve and look at different ways of writing; there the teacher of the course introduced me to the autoethnographic method, and she encouraged me to pursue it. Then luckily my supervisors were on board with this perspective.

Autoethnography could be understood within a broad philosophical field, from hermeneutics to phenomenology and existentialism. We can understand autoethnography as a springboard to foster the self and to make sure everyone's voice is heard. A method where subjectivity is at the centre of reflection. Every voice is equal. Autoethnography can be seen as an approach suitable for a type of writing based on examples,[59] as the idea behind the book-experience. Moreover, I would like to consider autoethnography as an approach capable of questioning power structure, and society, as an anarchist space of expression.

Autoethnography is a *telling* methodology. It has been conceptualized with the aim to recognize the limitations of scientific knowledge within humanities. This telling methodology gives appreciation to personal narrative and stories, as well as literary aesthetic emotions and insights. When autoethnographers tell stories, they use their own experiences to engage themselves and the circumstances. It is then correct to assume that the personal experience of the researcher is used to describe a certain reality, a circumstance. If we attune with the path of autoethnographers, when we retell our experiences, we can reframe our thinking, research or practice, together with our lives.[60] While autobiography and autoethnography are similar concepts, they are not the same. Nevertheless, Demetrio's ideas about autobiography can enhance our understanding of autoethnography to some extent. In describing what autobiography is, Demetrio states:

> Autobiography is not just a return to living: it is a return to growing for oneself and others, it is an encouragement to continue stealing days from the future that remains to us, and to live more profoundly, helped by that necessary and weaver self-made more vigilant by time and by those experiences that, due to the haste and carelessness of the crucial years, could not be lived with the same intensity. This is why autobiography is a formative journey and not a closure of accounts. Nonetheless, the revelation that we have been many selves can only push us to continue doing as much as we are given and for as long as we strive to complete our quest, our life.[61]

I understand this twofold. On one side there is a praxis which encourages us, the educators, to act and reflect in order to make sense of our educational practices. On the other side, there is a connection with the *a-methodic method* proposed by Mortari, and which I could relate to Ortega y Gasset's concept of *circumstancia:* autoethnography gives us the possibility to look at the world around us and reflect on it.

As Ellis then suggests, human life is messy and uncertain, and this of course should lead autoethnographer to a method that is capable of welcoming this *messiness.* Autoethnography seeks to reposition the researcher within the research process, acknowledging the inherent complexity. Therefore, I suggest that as educators we could adopt a research method that earnestly acknowledges and accommodates messiness, chaos, uncertainty, and emotion to the best of our ability.[62]

Likewise, autoethnography tries to avoid the standard use of colonialist and invasive ethnographic practices as it aims to not disregard the host culture. In my case for example, since I have been part of the early childhood education culture for a long time, I might probably speak with a voice that is closer to the stories described. These stories seek to give a representation of *a reality,* among *many others.* It is a representation of my reality as an educator, a reality that cannot give a general perspective, but to which one could partially relate to and then reframe it. Walford argues that "personal stories necessarily involve and depend upon others. It is thus possible to learn about the general from the particular."[63]

Moreover, as a researcher, it is possible to use pieces of my circumstances as articles, images, and every crumb that provides a sparkle of reflection. In this regard Ellis states that "it became necessary and desirable to recognize that we are part of what we study and, as researchers, to show how we are shaped and affected by our fieldwork experiences".[64] Thus, it is important to consider *the other* in our description, but how much can an autoethnographer write about the other? In this dissertation I have complied to my perspective, but I have not given clear suggestion on who or where certain facts happened. The people enclosed in my narration have been framed in general categories like "colleagues" or "children". I did it because I wanted to respect the people involved in it, as they could not give their consent. And whenever a name of a child is mentioned, for example when I quote my journals, the name has been made fictitious.

Autoethnographers, through the narration of their researches and experiences, create a relationship between past and present, writers and readers, tellers and audience. It is important to remember that autoethnographers present *one reality* among many others, and this reality is offered not only to the inner circle of academia but also to non-academic audiences.[65]

This method aims to unveil the ontology of the subject and the object. Ellis, Denzin and Goodall then suggest that social science cannot leave out such *a particular* and personal experience with its baggage of experiences.[66] Auto-ethnographers should be understood as a part of what it is researched. It means that as researchers we cannot relegate elements of our lives or experiences to the periphery. This is also what Zambrano proposes with her philosophy: to give the possibility to everyone to be heard[67]. Moreover, Ellis states:

> I did not believe in the silencing of voice that we required to produce the so-called proper academic subjectivities nor did I think that the worst sin I could commit as a researcher was to be too personal. I valued the personal and I wanted to include even to feature it in my work.[68]

It has been stated that the one who proposed the idea of *philosophical life* was Walter Kohan and, in the same way, Ellis argues that "doing autoethnography is more than a research method it is a way of living".[69] Autoethnographers offer insights into how it is possible to provide a perspective that others can use to make sense of similar experiences.[70] As it has been said, writing about the self always involves writing about others, when we write as an inquiry, we open a way of coming to know an experience better or differently.[71]

Sara Worth proposes the idea of *narrative knowledge* as a special form of reasoning.[72] Worth argues that the forms of knowledge that produce a *knowing how* and *knowing that* miss an important part, which is the *knowing what it is like.* Through stories, we have been given the possibility to get in touch with a knowledge that is rooted in empathy, which can lead us to an imaginative process in the understanding and meaning of what we read. In a perspective of storytelling, this approach fosters the practice of imagination.

Goodall understands Worth's insight in this way: when we write or tell a story, there is a connection between the teller and the listener. The very act of writing a story changes not so much how or what we know, it alters the way we think about it.[73] It is correct to assume that narratives are our way of knowing something, we tell stories in order to keep on living. So why can't we write research through a compelling narrative? One of the arguments used against autoethnography or every kind of narrative-based research is that the writer, the researcher, in doing this kind of work, loses objectivity. Goodall, instead, insists that we construct *a truth*, meaning that there is more than one truth. We represent a reality, we don't reproduce it.[74] So, it is important to consider autoethnography as a narration and as an attempt to embody life experiences.

Autoethnographers also consider the reader's perspective, acknowledging that a narrative's significance can vary depending on the reader's interpretation. This dynamic underscore a reciprocal relationship; it's not solely the researcher who shapes the narrative and constructs a particular reality, but the reader also possesses the authority and capability to evaluate the usefulness of a research.[75]

De Leon notices that according to indigenous scholars "stories have played a vital role in transmitting knowledge and teaching about common histories, past accomplishments, and cultural lessons".[76] To view autoethnography through the lenses of anarchism, De Leon suggests and argues that it is not about striving for a singular truth, but rather embracing it as a daily practice. Many scholars perceive the autoethnographic endeavour as a mean of resisting standardization and replication, thus advocating for diversity and autonomy in narrative construction.[77] Ellis, Denzin, Goodall also emphasize that it is important to write every day in order to keep a critical-reflexive practice in training.[78] It is so essential because as anarchist educators that try to resist standardization and replication in our practice, we have to reflect on this educational practice itself. De Leon underlines how anarchism confronts coercive institutions and hierarchies, experiencing them in ways that resonate within autoethnographic accounts, as they transcend discourses of objectivity. Documenting our experiences not only offers therapeutic benefits but also identifies oppressive social norms.[79]

Therefore, autoethnography represents a narrative focused on personal reflection. Within this understanding I can relate anarchism and autoethnography, both are marginal in the academia, both seek to move beyond something taken for granted that is built on hierarchical truths. They encourage subjectivity over objectivity and moreover the idea and practice of a collective and shared work.

In the next chapter I delve into the method drawn from Luigina Mortari's reading of Maria Zambrano, which I have reconceptualized as *w/o/a/ndering*.

Notes

[25] Mortari, Luigina. *Un Metodo a-Metodico.* (Napoli: Liguori Editore, 2006). I could also add from the same author, *A Scuola di Libertà.* (Milano: Raffaello Cortina Editore, 2008).

[26] Ingold, Tim. *The Life of Lines.* (New York: Routledge, 2015).

[27] Kohan, Walter. *El Maestro Inventor. Simón Rodríguez.* (Buenos Aires: Mino y Davila, 2018).

[28] Kohan, Walter. *Viajar Para Vivir: ensayar.* (Buenos Aires: Mino y Davola, 2015).

[29] Furthermore, other authors, like Rebecca Solnit 2001, Tim Ingold 2007, 2008, 2015 and Jan Masschelein 2010 have been important in developing this idea. I can also suggest the work the children of Reggio Emilia do and that is possible to see in some of their publications, 2008a, 2008b.

[30] Melanzini, Carla. *Insegnare al Principe di Danimarca.* (Palermo: Sellerio, 2023).

[31] See Walter Kohan's *Paulo Freire: a Philosophical Biography.* (London: Bloomsbury, 2021).

[32] Kohan 2021, p.93.

[33] Mortari 2006.

[34] Kohan 2021.

[35] Melanzini 2023.

[36] Ortega y Gasset, Josè. *Historia Como Sistema y Otros Ensayos de Filosofia.* (Alianza editorial, 2003).

[37] Mortari 2008.

[38] See for example Tim Ingold 2007, 2008, 2015; Luigina Mortari 2006, 2008.

[39] Ingold 2015.

[40] Ingold 2015, p.11.

[41] Ingold 2015, p.157.

[42] See Walter Kohan 2006, 2013, 2014b.

[43] McCarthy, Cormac. *La strada.* (Torino: Einaudi, 2006), p.64.

[44] Freire, Paulo. *Pedagogia dell'Autonomia.* (Torino: Gruppo Abele, 2014c).

[45] Freire 1990, 2014c.

[46] Wozniak, Jason. Introduction. In *The Inventive Schoolmaster.* Kohan, Walter. (Rotterdam, Sense publisher, 2015), p.xii.

[47] See Ward 1978, 1995, 2018.

[48] Zambrano, Maria. *Note di un Metodo.* (Napoli: Filema, 2003).

[49] Kohan, Walter. *Childhood, Education and Philosophy.* (New York: Routledge, 2015).

[50] Kohan 2015, p.xiii.

[51] Kohan 2015, p.22.

[52] Illich, Ivan. *Nella Vigna del Testo, per una Etologia della Lettura.* (Milano: Cortina, 1994).

[53] Henderson, Elizabeth. *Autoethnography in Early Childhood Education and Care, Narrating the Heart of Practice.* Routledge: New York: Routledge, 2018.

[54] Henderson 2018.

[55] Henderson 2018, p.85.

[56] Ortega y Gasset, Josè. *Meditations on Quixote.* (New York: The Norton library, 1963).

[57] Davies, Bronwyn and Gannon, Susanne. *Doing Collective Biography.* (London: Open University Press, 2006).

[58] Mollenhauer, Klaus. *Forgotten Connections.* (New York: Routledge, 2016), p.2.

[59] Hållander, Marie. *Det Omöjliga Vittnandet.* (Eskaton: Malmö: Eskaton, 2017).

[60] Mortari, Luigina. *Cultura della Ricerca e Pedagogia.* (Roma: Carocci, 2007).

[61] Demetrio, Duccio. *Raccontarsi, l'Autobiografia come Cura di sé.* (Milano: Cortina, 1996), p.16.

[62] Ellis, Carolyn & al. *Autoethnography. Understanding Qualitative Research.* (Oxford: Oxford University Press, 2015), p.9.

[63] Walford, Geoffrey. Finding the Limits: Autoethnography and Being an Oxford University proctor. 403–417. *Qualitative Research*, 4 (3). 2004, p.412.

[64] Ellis & al. 2015, p.10.

[65] See for example the work of Ellis & al. 2015; Denzin, 2019, 2014; Goodall 2000, 2019; Bochner 1997.

[66] See for example the work of Ellis & al. 2015; Denzin, 2019, 2014; Goodall 2000, 2019; Bochner 1997.

[67] Mortari 2006, 2019.

[68] Ellis & al. 2015, p.9.

[69] Ellis & al. 2015, p.20.

[70] Ellis & al. 2015, p.27.

[71] Ellis & al. 2015, p.56.

[72] Worth, Sara. Storytelling and Narrative Knowing: An Examination of the Epistemic Benefits of well-told Stories. *The Journal of Aesthetic Education*, 42, p.42–56. 2008.

[73] Goodall, H.L. *Writing Qualitative Inquiry. Self, Stories and Academic Life.* (New York: Routledge, 2019).

[74] See for example the work of Ellis & al. 2015; Denzin, 2019, 2014; Goodall 2000, 2019; Bochner 1997.

[75] See for example the work of Ellis & al. 2015; Denzin, 2019, 2014; Goodall 2000, 2019; Bochner 1997.

[76] DeLeon, Abraham P. How Do I Begin To Tell a Story that Has Not Been Told? Anarchism, Autoethnography, and the Middle Ground, in *Equity & Excellence in Education*, 2010, 398–413, 43:4, p.399

[77] DeLeon 2010, p.403.

[78] See for example the work of Ellis & al. 2015; Denzin, 2019, 2014; Goodall 2000, 2019; Bochner 1997.

[79] DeLeon 2010, p.410.

Walking . . . is how the body measures itself against the earth.
And a path is a prior interpretation of the best way to traverse a landscape.
Rebecca Solnit

Caminante, no hay camino, se hace camino al andar.
Antonio Machado

Above all, do not lose your desire to walk.
I have walked myself into my best thoughts,
I know of no thought so burdensome that one cannot walk away from it.
If one just keeps on walking, everything will be all right.
Søren Kierkegaard

CHAPTER THREE

W/o/a/ndering:
Luigina Mortari's reading of Maria Zambrano

The Italian scholar and philosopher Luigina Mortari will be our travelling companion in these pages. Mortari's work *Un metodo a-metodico* is grounded in the reading of Maria Zambrano's work, a Spanish philosopher of the 20th century.[80] Zambrano's writing reminds me of fragments, scratches in the soul of the reader. It is not systemic, she writes about many different topics,[81] and her thought takes the reader on a journey for the mind and the soul.[82] This is also a w/o/a/ndering approach to philosophy. In this chapter I illustrate the method suggested by Mortari, and I intend to follow the path she traced.

When we choose to become educators, there is a reason that drives us to make this choice. To choose to educate is to choose to open oneself, to give oneself to the other. To choose to educate is to face the question Zambrano poses "What to do?"[83] With this question, Zambrano underlines how the educational practice is ontologically problematic, because according to the philosopher, no one has the answer.[84]

Mortari, thus, underlines that there is a need for pedagogy to firmly reconnect with philosophy since life has always been the object of philosophy. Philosophy in this sense must be seen as a bridge between life and thought that helps beings to live life with meaning[85]. Educational practice needs to converse with a philosophy based on the experience of life, a philosophy which questions our experience.[86] For this reason, it is necessary to look for a philosophy that can become a companion in our errancy, an a-methodological-philosophical approach to education.

My first encounter with Maria Zambrano was during my philosophy of education course through Luigina Mortari's book *Un Metodo a-Metodico*.[87] Mortari's reflections profoundly marked and helped me change my practice as an educator and my approach to everyday life. An aspect that is sometimes underestimated. I find it difficult to separate these two sides, as the personal influences the educational practice, and vice versa.

The poetic essence of Zambrano's writing has always been fascinating and her constant reflection on the meaning of life is a theme that has always involved me deeply. A philosophical-poetic reflection that gave an important contribution to Spanish culture and this is the reason why she won the Cervantes Prize, the Nobel Prize for literature in Spanish language.

The counter-current life experience Zambrano followed is another aspect I took in consideration for this thesis. A woman who was an academic in a strongly patriarchal culture such as Spain was at the time. The idea and practice of helping the outcast of society through literacy programs. The struggle to defend the Spanish Republic from the Francoists. The subsequent exile. All of these experiences can be read in her philosophy where the search for being, circumstances and openness to the other are fundamental themes.

Zambrano incorporates in her philosophical proposal other concepts already analyzed by various scholars such as the ontological place of being, truth, feeling, time and the epochè.[88] However, it is the way in which she approaches these concepts that make her philosophy so compelling. Zambrano proposes an understanding of these concepts through one's own experience, she invites the reader to feel these concepts through experience. This is a way, as Mortari then suggests, that should be the modus operandi of the philosopher of education, "to grasp those aspects of philosophical discourse that allow us to pinpoint the essence of education and to outline its problematic aspects, and then to propose possible courses of action".[89] Thus, the constant search for being is the basis on which Mortari and Zambrano's philosophical and pedagogical thinking is founded.

As it has been said before, I mainly refer to the reading that Mortari does of Zambrano's work, as in it I have found a philosophical link between the various concepts that I lay out in this thesis. This reading will give a philosophical understanding of autoethnography, anarchism, storytelling or story play, or reflections about pedagogical documentation.

To better place this method, I am going to display a fragment, an event that took place some time ago when I worked as an educator in an early childhood care center. Later on, I will analyse it through Mortari's proposal and my idea of w/o/a/ndering. The event presented in the fragment is a good example on how I used the compass *received* by Mortari. Finally, I would like to think to this a-method, and to a way to be an anarchist educator.

A fragment about a birch wood

I was recently returning home from my photographic walk when I found a yellow envelope inside the mailbox. The handwriting was familiar and a long time had passed since I last saw it. In the envelope there was a small sheet of paper with greetings and a second envelope with some photographs of me when I worked in a children's education center.

I still remember that year. Above all, I remember a project, born by chance, that taught me so much as an educator. By the way, I really like the term project as it reminds me of the gerund idea of being, something in the making. When we project, we look ahead. This runs counter to the idea of the method that Zambrano, as we shall see, proposes. That is why I understand the project as looking into the future, a project as a process, an open w/o/a/ndering and not a path towards a final goal.

It took me some time to come to this understanding. At the beginning of my career as an educator in early childhood education, the project was just a final product to be given to the parents.

In any case, it had been a difficult year for several reasons. And even if we were doing our best, I recognize that our ability to listen to children and to ourselves had diminished. We were in what I could call a self-pilot mode. The projects we carried out were made for the children, but not with the children. I was dissatisfied with myself. Disappointed. Demoralized. I admit that I had no mental and emotional energy to turn the situation around.

With this mindset, my colleagues and I embarked on a new project, intending it to last until the beginning of the summer. A safe passage waiting for better times.

We were near the end of the school year and we wanted to conclude it with one last project. But which one? As always, we tried to listen to the children, to their interests. It wasn't easy, they were a mine of different ideas and interests. A couple of colleagues, however, proposed a project on portraits and self-portraits. The idea came about because observing the children, we noticed they had an interest in the photographs hanging in the classroom where they were portrayed, in how they mirrored themselves on every available surface. To be fair, not all of them were interested in this. However, we thought it was enough to justify our project. Over the next few days, we educators began to collect materials, to prepare and start the project. At that time, there was an art exhibition in an open gallery space where reproductions of famous contemporary artists such as Picasso, Modigliani, Schiele, Klimt, and more modern ones such as Rembrandt, Goya and Vermeer, were on display. I do not remember exactly all of the artists, but what made the exhibition unique was how the paintings were divided in different categories, such as portraits, nature, war and so on. This subdivision also had a common thread, the human being, and his environment, i.e. the world. For example, the portraits were meant to show the equality and at the same time the uniqueness of human beings, the nature theme was meant to talk about respect for the environment around us, and so on. What better occasion for our project, a visit to the exhibition center would have, at least in our minds, sparked the children's interest.

And so, we got to the day of the visit. In my head, I was already picturing the enraptured gaze of the children at the exhibit. I imagined a riot of happiness, of curiosity. We entered. The first room was dedicated to war, then nature, and gradually the other rooms, until we almost reached the end of the exhibition, where we found the much-desired portraits. Before leaving to return to school we suggested going back inside to see the portrait room again, to get some more inspiration and take some photographs of the paintings. However, several children asked to go back and see the first two rooms, but as we were there for the portraits and had little time, we said no. The day was over. We were happy with the trip, everything seemed to have gone according to plan.

The next day it was time to start our project and we sat in a circle and started talking, asking, listening, what they had seen the day before, and what they had liked best in the portraits. What they wanted to do. The answers were not exactly what we expected or wanted to hear. In short, the jubilation of happiness, and the rapt looks I had fantasised about were not there. While leafing through the book, however, two intentions clashed. On the one hand we educators were trying to show the paintings we considered important for our project, on the other hand the children were looking for paintings they found interesting to explore. One way or another, however, we educators always managed to return to the paintings we had already chosen for the project.

Over the next few days, the project finally took off. We worked hard to complete the activity, to give a completed craft before the end of school, a small portfolio with several portraits inspired by the visit to the exhibition center. Those days were difficult. The children were not interested in the work proposed. We educators were stressed as we had to 'produce' something to hand in, to show the parents that we were working. Time passed and there was frustration in the group. No one was happy. We needed to discuss it.

"But what are we doing?" I asked my colleagues. It was clear to me that we had lost our bearings a bit, there was no cohesion. What I did know, however, was that we weren't really listening. We had imposed a project, 'our' project, based on some observations made on the group, but without really asking. It

was in that very moment that I realised that we were lazy educators. Educators who had no desire to research, to listen, to support the children. We were just educators who wanted to 'copy' projects seen in manuals because they were 'aesthetically' beautiful, but we weren't critical thinkers. With these remarks, I do not want to make it look worse than it was. The children came to the education center willingly every single morning, they did not want to go home in the afternoon, when they met me around town, they always greeted me, and the parents were happy. The project itself was going on and the children were talking about it with their parents in a positive way. However, there seemed to be a lack of that playfulness that was present at other times of the year, in other projects. But how and what to do then? The solution was the simplest, to sit around the bonfire and talk to those directly involved: the children. This so-called bonfire was a round red carpet we had in the classroom on which we sat in a circle. The bonfire gave us a setting to envision ourselves in a forest, where we could engage in open conversations, philosophical discussions, and story-telling, sharing anecdotes, facts, or questions. It was a sharing space.

The next day we sat around the bonfire.

Me: *"Children, do you like the portrait project?"*

The answers were varied, although some were negative, most were positive, but not enthusiastic.

Child: *I don't think I want to paint myself; I am not good at it.*

Me: *Well, what does it mean to be good? We can try to draw and paint.*

Child: *But maybe it becomes a strange drawing and the other children will make fun of me.*

Me: *I understand, but I don't think that it will happen.*

Child: *are you sure?*

This was a good question; I didn't know how to answer since I could not promise such a thing. So, I changed direction.

Me: *"What would you like to do then? Did you see something in the exhibition that made you think?"*

Silence.

A child stood up and picked up the book with all the paintings on display. He leafed through it, back and forth and forward again. He stopped. He pointed his finger. "This one!" he said.

It was Picasso's Guernica.

Me: *"How come? Do you know what it represents?" I asked.*

A child answered: "The gentleman who was explaining things (the guide), said it is a war."

"Yes exactly," I replied.

From then on, the discussion opened to the whole group, and we talked about wars, why they exist, whether it is right or wrong to start them, and so on. The discussion went on for a while until it was time for other activities. At the end of the day we met again, thinking we could start with Picasso's painting and explore some of the themes the children had investigated during the day. However, we were more aware that perhaps it was another attempt of ours to engage in another project, half-listening. We decided to wait until the following day and see how the discussion would evolve. The risk in this case is thinking that you own the children.

The day after another child asked if he could show us a painting. Klimt's The Birch Forest. I asked why, what it was that attracted him, and what made him think of. "To peace and a fantasy full world," he said. Hard to reply. I remember when I saw it for the first time at the Belvedere in Vienna, I was enchanted and stared at it for several minutes, immersing myself in that forest with my imagination. The children seemed really interested, they started asking a lot of questions about the forest, fantasizing about the inhabitants, and telling 'stories'. It was as if the embers within each of us had been rekindled to make a beautiful fire. The forest could be seen as a place of fantasy, of imagination, how many stories have a forest as their backdrop? I consider it the place of a thousand possibilities. Like those of children. And like them, we educators could also have a memory of our past as children by putting ourselves at stake.

Another day over and another meeting. We had decided to meet more often so that we could plan our days better, they were not working hours, we did it on a voluntary basis, because being educators was not just a job, it was also a bit of a mission and sometimes you have to give a bit of your time for free. We were already imagining what project we could do, we had books and manuals to inspire us. We were still making the same mistake, proposing our own project. There was a catch. How could we propose a common project, where every child could really be involved? A project that could also be 'handed over' to the parents. The idea came when I thought about my own experience as a relational psychomotor therapist, when we used to tell stories in our room.

When we tell stories, collectively, we are actors and audience at the same time. We create a collective narration. We create a scene that, as in a theatre, can provide infinite possibilities of expression. There was a room in the education center that was not used at that time, it also had a beautiful glass window, and it was connected to the garden outside. We covered all the walls with white paper, from the ceiling to the floor, then hung a colour photocopy of Klimt's painting. The idea was simply to leave it to the children. We gave them space, we gave them help, we put ourselves at stake, but above all we left, or tried to leave, a possibility always open to becoming. They had the chance to decorate the space as they wished, to use different materials they found or desired so to develop their artistic projects or to play, or even to tell stories. Within the limits of material availability, they could access any possibility. As I have already said, the room was empty, this gave the opportunity to the children to w/o/a/nder in their imagination. In addition, the children could document their w/o/anderings with us. This also gave us the chance to do two things, to document in order to include the parents in our work, and above all to document what the children felt was important to show. We, educators, didn't decide what to document.

Around the bonfire, we presented our intention and before we started, we shared a few rules. The children entered the room. It looked like a room in some spaceship. Completely white. A single painting on the wall. A large box with different materials to create, draw and colour. This was what we were offering at the time, but as educators, we were more aware of the value of listening and accommodating any requests, such as when one child asked to be allowed to use some games, or when others asked to go for a trip to the nearby forest in order to collect materials they could use in their fictive-forest. Over the next few days, that room became an artistic-creative workshop, where stories intertwined, where every idea was considered. The forest expanded to the garden, to some other parts of the educational center. It was no longer just a great graphic expression, but it had become a stage, where the children told more and more stories through play. We, educators, were not just observers but actors like and with the children. There were of course also moments of frustration, misunderstanding and anger, but also moments where the children together found solutions to their problems.

W/o/a/ndering as an *a-posteriori* method

Mortari writes that for Zambrano life is like a rushing river.[90] Although I am comfortable with this metaphor, at the same time I think of another image related to another painting. The 1818 painting by Caspar David Friedrich, *Der Wanderer Uber dem Nebelmeer*. It depicts a wanderer with his back turned observing from a summit the mountains below him enveloped in clouds that shape as a sea (*Nebelmeer*).

A peculiarity of Friedrich's painting is the presence of what in German is called a *Rückenfigur,* i.e. a person, in this case, the subject of the painting, depicted from behind. A person absorbed in contemplation. A wayfarer who, after wandering along paths and mountains, now wanders and wonders in his thoughts. Through the *Rückenfigur* technique, the viewer identifies with the character portrayed, making it easier to enter the painting.

This painting evokes in me the *a-methodical method* proposed by Mortari, as well as the philosophical approach of Zambrano. I understand the wayfarer as a metaphor: the way we are in relation to life. Allow me to extend this metaphor. I think of this wayfarer as an educator, as a parent. This educator/wanderer, being on top of a mountain shall not be interpreted as an omniscient, oppressive educator. It should be understood as an educator and, why not, even an educatee who scans the horizon to get his or her bearings, in the difficulties, in the unforeseen events that lurk behind the clouds. We cannot know the future. But we can imagine it. The future is a possibility, like what anarchism praises. The landscape is covered by clouds, and only when we get closer can we discover a little more of our path. The wayfarer should also pay attention to sounds, each sound or voice can lead him or her on a different path. As educators or learners, we often find ourselves navigating our paths step by step, gradually revealing our journey.[91] This is why I find storytelling to be such a captivating educational tool. When we engage in storytelling, we immerse ourselves in narratives that unfold like mountain ridges among the clouds, offering countless possibilities. Just as we cannot predict their destinations, we must ascend these paths, finding our way through the unknown.[92]

This reflection outlined above can be found in the fragment of the woods. It can be reread as follows: as an educator, I have not been like the wayfarer, I have not listened, and not looked to the educational horizon. As an educator I have looked at my own feet, keeping my head down. The wayfarer keeps his or her head up to look at possible destinations. A wayfarer who, as an educator, should not only wander physically but should also wander in spirit, an educator who lives in gerundive.

Another consideration about the episode displayed. When we entered for the first time in the white room, we were wayfarers, both children and us. We w/o/a/ndered out and about all the possibilities we had in that space, it was no longer a *room* but a *new world to create and contemplate.* Just a remark here, one could think that if you look at your feet you are looking at your *circunstancia.* I disagree with this perspective. In this instance, you appear self-absorbed, failing to consider the circumstances. By looking around, you can truly appreciate your surroundings.[93] My role as an educator in that room closely aligned with my vision of educational anarchism. We simply prepared the space – a protected environment – where both children and adults could gather and explore themselves, fostering a sense of freedom and a journey inward.

Mortari says that our becoming is a continuous coming into being, which is a human *proprium*[94], then according to Zambrano "to live humanly is to come into being".[95] In these insights we can notice not only the educational experience from the perspective of the educator but also from the point of view of the child or educatee. In my experience as an educator, I understand this rebirth on a daily basis, just like when children tell stories that are continuously reinterpreted, and the same story is transformed day after day. In role-playing, children and educators have the possibility to be reborn in other guises. But it is not easy to put oneself out there, we metaphorically take off our clothes, leaving our certainties behind to enter a world unknown to us. It takes courage to do this. However, it is important to be reminded of our role as educators. In other words, we do not stop educating even if by 'play' we become something else. I did this as an educator when proposing the Birch Wood Project with my colleagues, I was leaving my certainties, and I didn't know what could have happened in that room. A room that allowed children to create and tell stories, that for some aspect it was like the room where I worked as therapist some years before. A space where educators and children could *become* through w/o/a/ndering, where there were no hierarchical relationships, rather horizontal ones. There finally was the possibility to enhance an educational practice between adults and children, an education done *with* (children), rather than *for* (children).[96]

Mortari emphasizes the necessity for pedagogy to grasp educational experience fully, transforming it into living knowledge. By delving into the experience of life itself, pedagogy evolves into experiential knowledge. Through rigorous questioning, theoretical thought is refined. Mortari then suggests that life has always been the subject of philosophy, underscoring the importance for pedagogy to reconnect firmly with its philosophical roots. This questioning/investigation of experience extends beyond tangible educational practices to the point that it includes intellectual engagement, such as reading and reflection.[97]

I interpret Mortari's passage as a crucial insight into an anarchist approach to education. Anarchism places particular emphasis on reflective engagement with practice. This poses a challenge in this dissertation, as understanding anarchism is best achieved through practical application. It's worth noting that many anarchist philosophers in education also have practical experience as educators themselves.

When I read, and it is not important if it is a philosophical or fictional book, my experience leads me to question myself. When I read some books to my children or to the children in the early childhood center, I can appreciate their response to the reading, I appreciate their questions, their ideas. Then when I am alone, I go through those pages again and I try to question myself as well. This can also happen when storyplay or storytelling occurs during the day, I usually play with children, I try to take notes on their discussions, and then at the end of the week I go through those dialogues to understand and tune myself to their voice. Malaguzzi said that we (adults) speak a lot *about* childhood and children, but not as much *with* them.[98] This is what happened before changing our approach and deciding to implement The Birch Wood project. Once we began to listen to children, the project developed and I believe that not only the children enjoyed it, but we did it too and we could also reflect on our growth as educators. In our practice it is important to write the reflections and the observations we have regarding education. It is important to read and to keep reading those observations. It is then correct to say that reading, as well as writing, is an experience. These insights should be thought as impressions, fleeting moments, and we should think of us as poets who interrogate life.[99] As Zambrano says:

> This philosophy is not that of the great systems, a philosophy that is distracted from the existential questions of everyday life. Philosophy can find a vital and necessary thought in less systematic forms of thought, in some cases closer to poetry and therefore closer to life.[100]

Mortari suggests that in everyday life, especially when there is an educational practice going on, we are called upon to give a direction of meaning.[101] This meaning can be a lot of things, for example cooperation, empathy, critical thinking. As an educator then I try to facilitate situations where these meanings are present or to show first-hand what a *meaning* means. If I aim to enhance empathy, I should show what it means to be empathic. For this reason, it is important to think to an educational practice in dialogue with a philosophy based on life experience that at the same time questions our experience.

Furthermore, Zambrano in *Delirio e Destino* takes up Ortega y Gasset's concept that living is co-living,[102] and she suggests that "the other is the companionship that every being needs".[103] According to Mortari "to live alone is to live in the middle".[104] In these propositions a common thread emerges, a thread that is developed in both their philosophy: the idea of collectivity. We need companionship. Mortari suggests "the journey of life is not a path that each person takes alone, but always with others. Without the other, the journey does not produce a real movement".[105] In other words we should not think of ourselves as atoms isolated in space, but as atoms coming together to form our experiences. Autoethnography or anarchism encourage us to think and walk within this horizon.

As an educator, but also as a father, I can't imagine myself to educate alone, for two reasons. One, if I am alone, who am I going to educate? Two, we live in a society, this means that we have relationships to look after, and in order to take care of these relationships, freedom needs to be guaranteed. Anarchism, in its ontology, grants this freedom and we have seen that freedom means to create spaces where others can show themselves, it means to foster individuality, not to oppress other's will. Thus, we need an approach that opens up to unexpected possibilities.

Zambrano writes in *Note di un Metodo* that "true experience cannot be given without the intervention of some sort of method".[106] She proposes a method that is not *a-priori* but *a-posteriori*.[107] There is no method in principle to get to know life, because life is unrepeatable, its situations are unique.[108] An a-priori method would take away the possibility of experience and we should adapt to the method itself. One could say that experience is a-priori, while the method is a-posteriori. It's not so straight. When we experience, simultaneously we are also constructing the method, and this helps us give meaning to that experience. Method and experience are intertwined. It's not far from what anarchist education encourages educators to do. A method is a path to be walked one or more times, and Zambrano encourages us to be courageous on this path, we must let ourselves be carried along by the unexpected.[109]

As an anarchist educator I need to be able to see things, and circumstances, from different points of view and I need to adapt mentally to do so. I also need to be an example of what I preach. I am reminded of the sculptor who walks around the piece of marble ready to be carved, or the photographer who changes lenses or position before taking a photo to find a different perspective. Referring to the fragments at the beginning of this chapter, when we educators planned the whole activity, we had done so by placing ourselves a-priori to the educational practice. Later when we had "lost our way" after we had experienced it, and reflected on it, we found it back again. We proposed an educational practice *with* children rather than *for* children. Plasticity is important because it gives us the mental state to adapt to the situation.

Picture books as an (anarchist) w/o/a/ndering experience

Reading a picture book allows educators and children to w/o/a/nder. A picture book allows educators and children to critically engage from other perspectives. It is possible, thus, to consider a picture book as Mortari could propose, an object to be investigated from several perspectives.[110]

Colin Ward looked at playgrounds as an anarchist parable, I look at picture books as an anarchist parable.[111] There are some books that could be interpreted more than others within an anarchist understanding. *Alice in Wonderland* is an example but also *Where the Wild things are*, *Winnie the Pooh* or some Shaun Tan's books, like *The Lost Thing*. Moreover, these books also foster the concept of w/o/a/ndering.

These reflections have grown over the years, reading the works of other educators and scholars such as those of Joanna Haynes or Karin Murris and others who also use picture books to promote philosophy with children.[112] Undoubtedly my approach to discover picture books is strongly influenced by philosophy with children, but it is precisely the w/o/a/ndering approach that comes into play. Above all, these reflections arose after my experience with the Birch Wood and the philosophical-educational meeting with Luigina Mortari. As an educator, I give great attention to reading or telling stories, however at the beginning I had just one perspective, one voice, which was my own. Being an educator is a growing process, a w/o/a/ndering, a becoming.

What about picture books as a parable of anarchism and w/o/a/ndering?

Picture books are w/o/a/ndering books. Stories, drawings, journeys are important elements of these kind of books, and so are the reflections these stories bring. I am thinking for example of Tan's book *The Arrival*, which reflects on what it means to be an immigrant. A much-discussed theme in recent years, seeing the great mass of human beings who are forced to leave their homes, often displaced in unbearable situations, where the West shows its hypocrisy hesitating between welcoming and rejecting them. The stories often depicted in picture books, like the ones afore mentioned, are also stories of resistance, stories that create collective narration, stories that could tune with an approach based on anarchism.

The story I often used to read as a child and, overall, as an educator was and still is Winnie the Pooh by A. A. Milne. From a strictly educational point of view, in this book I find precisely the sense of w/o/a/ndering that I am explaining in this chapter, as well as perspectives on the horizon of anarchism. First, the story (the stories if one also considers the later versions, the various spin-offs), takes place within the Hundred Acre Wood. I am suggesting to see this wood as a microcosmos of anarchism. In this forest each protagonist is independent and autonomous, and wanders through it. All the characters: Pooh, Piglet, Eeyore, Tigger, Rabbit, Owl, Kanga with her son Roo, live in harmony without a centralised authority. Everyone can seek their own individuality, their own way of being, like Pooh and his perpetual search for honey. Each character is bound by voluntary relationships and friendship, which turns into mutual aid and collaboration. In this equality I find Kanga's position to be quite interesting, as she is a mother who raises her son Roo alone. A position that challenges traditional gender roles. Finally, I understand Milne's work as an intertwining between w/o/a/ndering and anarchism, the author celebrates children's creativity, play and innate sense of curiosity in his writing. I find a sense of resistance in the writing, where this portrayal of the heroes makes adults reflect on how we sometimes have certain expectations and rules imposed by society and how we should instead embrace the character's playful endeavors.

When I read this book in the classroom, I realised how children perceived the characters as their playmates. Certainly, the fact that Tigger, Piglet and all the others can also be found as *playmates* on shops' shelves helps in making it more concrete. I usually read one chapter a week, so that space and time are dilated, and it is then possible to see what comes out of this reading. I always try, together with the children, to recreate a forest of our own inside the school, or if possible, in the garden or in a neighboring forest. In the stories mentioned, and in others, I am thinking for example about Narnia or Harry Potter, there is always this magical side of places parallel to reality (or maybe it is we that live in an unreal world?), a place that attracts children, and adults, because they are places of possibility, of imagination. In these places it is also possible to think about new experiences, to encourage w/o/a/ndering, and to see how educational practice unfolds, a practice that, as it has been said, cannot be anticipated.

As an educator, therefore, I certainly must present some possibilities for exploration, but how this possibility is received and developed by the children remains unexpected. I always think that the educator has two choices in presenting these w/o/a/ndering possibilities, on the one hand he can do it from his own idea, on the other hand he can do it by listening attentively to the children. Neither is easy. The risk of overstepping is always lurking around the corner. When we read a picture book (and develop maybe another activity from the reading) we could think of Zambrano when she invites us not to stay in an anticipated world, because we risk not to paying attention to otherness.[113] To do this we are called to leave aside our prejudices and open ourselves to the encounter.

I always try to keep this predisposition in mind, especially when I enter new environments and educational contexts. And here an image comes to mind. The empty room with the reproduction of Klimt's painting, of the forest described in the fragment at the beginning. An empty room invites encounter, without distractions of any kind, everyone can become aware of themselves and find a way to create a collective experience. Children and we educators without predefined objects in the room can express ourselves freely without conditioning. Mortari insists on the fact of continuous rebirth, of transformation, which is what Zambrano defines a shipwreck and I understand as a w/o/a/ndering.[114]

In Mortari and Zambrano's philosophical and poetical understanding of the human being's condition I was able to find the way of being an anarchist educator, but above all I also found an attitude that I seek in my practice as an educator. In these pages, therefore, I have reproposed, albeit partially, a philosophical approach to education according to Mortari. An approach that can be seen as the red thread of this thesis, an approach that aims at the realisation of a democratic world, where everyone can be a fulfilled being. A world where differences are harmonized. While Mortari offers us a philosophy of hope, Zambrano wants to give voice to all that remains in the shadows.

Notes

[80] Mortari, Luigina. *Un Metodo a-Metodico, la Pratica della Ricerca in Maria Zambrano.* (Napoli: Liguori, 2006).

[81] Mortari, Luigina. *Maria Zambrano.* (Milano: Feltrinelli, 2019).

[82] Mortari 2019.

[83] Mortari 2006.

[84] Mortari 2006.

[85] Mortari 2006.

[86] Mortari 2006.

[87] Mortari 2006.

[88] Mortari 2019.

[89] Mortari 2006, p.8.

[90] Mortari 2006.

[91] Zambrano 1992, 1996; Mortari 2008.

[92] Mortari 2008.

[93] Zambrano, Maria. *Chiari del Bosco.* (Milano: Bruno Mondadori, 2004).

[94] Mortari 2006, 2008.

[95] Zambrano, Maria. *Sogno e Tempo.* (Bologna: Pendragon, 2004b), p.41.

[96] Korczak 2013a; Burke and Jones 2014; VV.AA. I cento linguaggi dei bambini 2010.

[97] Mortari 2006.

[98] Malaguzzi, Loris. *Loris Malaguzzi and the Schools of Reggio Emilia.* (edited by Cagliari, P., Castagnetti, M., et alt.). New York: Routledge, 2016.

[99] Mortari, 2006.

[100] Zambrano, Maria. *Verso un Sapere dell'Anima.* (Milano: Cortina, 1996), p.55.

[101] Mortari 2006.

[102] Zambrano, Maria. *Delirio e Destino.* (Milano: Cortina, 2000).

[103] Zambrano, Maria. *Note di un Metodo.* (Napoli: Filema, 2003). p.72.

[104] Mortari 2006, p.14.

[105] Mortari 2006, p.15.

[106] Zambrano 2003, p.35.

[107] Mortari 2006.

[108] Mortari 2006.

[109] Mortari 2006.

[110] Mortari 2006.

[111] Ward, Colin. *Anarchy in Action.* (Oakland: PM press, 2018).

[112] Haynes, Joanna and Murris, Karin. *Picturebooks, Pedagogy and Philosophy.* (New York: Routledge, 2012). Haynes, Joanna. *Children as Philosophers.* (New York: Routledge, 2008). In this context I can also mention the important contribution that Gareth Matthew gave to the field of Philosophy for Children and to my understanding of this educational practice. See Matthew 1980, 1984, 1994. These three books, introduced to me in a course of philosophy of education, gave the theoretical ground for my critical thinking about the possibilities of encounter with children and philosophy.

[113] Mortari 2006.

[114] Mortari 2006.

We think we tell stories, but stories often tell us, tell us to love or hate, to see
or be seen. Often, too often, stories saddle us, ride us, whip us onward, tell
us what to do, and we do it without questioning. The task of learning to be
free requires learning to hear them, to question them, to pause and hear
silence, to name them, and then become a storyteller.
Rebecca Solnit

The universe is made of stories, not of atoms.
Muriel Rukeyser

CHAPTER FOUR

Storytelling and/as education

"I would like to hear from you what storytelling is". This was a comment I got from a reader of my dissertation. A simple observation, with a not so easy answer. So, let's try to give an answer to this comment. Storytelling is a possibility. A place of imagination. A place of belonging. A place of anarchism. A place of w/o/a/ndering. Storytelling is an open and ever evolving dialogue that connects and relates human beings to each other and to the *circumstancia*. Children practice storytelling when they play through a story, and usually in children's play there is always a story involved. Storytelling is put into action when we read picture books, as we create a possibility to immerse ourselves in another world, and thus questions arise from this imaginary world. When we w/o/a/nder out and about with children and observe the world, we can imagine, we can play ... and these are moments of storytelling. When children go home from preschool and tell the parents about their day, there is an act of storytelling. These are but few examples of what storytelling could be.

In my childhood, stories have been a fundamental part of my growth. As a child I lived in the same villa with my grandparents, the stories that my grandfather told me, the attraction I had for his huge library made up of old books, was a perpetual engine of imagination. I remember my grandmother who patiently listened to my stories or participated in my pretend plays. Even when I moved out of my childhood's house I continued to live in a world of stories. Fortunately, as I became an adult, I did not lose this interest. Nowadays I play with my children, I look at picture books, photographic books, I take photos on daily bases, I write short stories when I can, or I tell stories to my children before they go to bed. I'm surrounded by stories.

Over time, in my educational practice, I have tried to develop an approach that looks at storytelling. Certainly, as I wrote in the introduction to this thesis, the push to further develop this interest and see the potential was given to me by my experience as a relational psychomotricist. In that context I understood how stories connect us, both the stories we tell in that moment, stories that we act through pretend play and build together with others, but also the stories already told, which become a common culture, a place where we can also return sometimes to feel safe, to feel our place of belonging. This is undoubtedly facilitated by the educational context of reference, that of early childhood education.

Thus, I suggest storytelling as a twofold possibility, from one side a space where educators and children can w/o/a/nder, on the other side a pocket to foster an anarchist practice. When as educators we engage in an approach based on storytelling, we can understand our relationship with children, our educational horizon, and we can understand ourselves as educators better.

As I did in the previous chapter, here I intertwine a more theoretical text with some practical examples from my experience as an educator. In the display of an experience, I had some years ago, I will reflect not only on the concept of storytelling, but also on the concept of anarchism and of w/o/-a/ndering.

When the children met Clay

Clay is a dear friend of mine. It has been following me for many years. We shared good times together. We went through several adventures. We met many children, many hands. We had fun. It can speak so many languages, it can understand everyone, mould itself in different ways. Oh, yes, I must mention that Clay is not a person, anyway not in the sense we normally think of a person. However, it does not matter, we include everyone and everything.

I have met Clay many times in my life, ever since I was a child, and I have always found it amusing and fascinating. As an educator I then got to know it better and it has become what I call possibility-connective, something that brings children, educators and the environment together, creating new possibilities. I think Clay is democratic and anarchic, as well as a great storytelling sidekick. It is Democratic because anyone can relate to it, and Clay likes to talk to anyone in their favourite language. Sure, there are children that don't like to touch Clay, its muddiness, but they can wait that clay is dry (for example it can be a figure to be painted) and play with it. It is anarchic because his relationship with the other is horizontal, not vertical. Clay likes to connect people, children and educators, and make them work together. In addition, his specialty is to create the conditions for free expression and thus an excellent space for creating one's own stories. Perhaps Clay is interested in the concept of w/o/a/ndering, as we will see in a moment.

In any case, a few years ago I had already started to look with an interest at anarchist practices in education, at its theorisation, and above all I already had some educational experience in my pockets. And here pockets are a valuable tool for educators, both metaphorical pockets and real pockets. We can put our experiences in the metaphorical pockets, our thoughts, our reflections, so that when needed we can rummage through these pockets and pull out something useful. In the real pockets, on the other hand, we can collect tools and objects useful for our educational practice and sometimes they become treasure chests where we can keep precious objects that children ask us to keep for a while. Back to Clay. At that time, I was lucky enough to work in a group of talented and competent educators and thus I had the opportunity to learn a lot. One colleague was interested in storytelling, play, and alternative forms of education just like me.

Due to my experience with the birch wood (cf. the chapter before), I knew that I did not want to impose any project to the children, but at the same time I also wanted to offer a chance to discover something new. These are always some of the issues I reflect on as an educator, how much I actually have to propose and how much space I have left for discovery. It also depends, of course, on the age of the children. So, we agreed on a plan. We put a block of clay on a wooden box placed on the floor, covered it with a light-coloured plastic so as to ignite curiosity, but at the same time without imposing a specific activity. I knew, having worked with clay many times before, that something would happen anyway, but what exactly remained to be seen.

The children began to ask what it was, they went around the thing, around the Clay. They were getting closer and closer. Now, don't think that they were intimidated, frightened by it (even though almost tens of kilos of clay are quite a lot), but they didn't really understand what it was, and especially what to do with it. Neither I nor my colleague had said anything about it. This curiosity was actually kindled not immediately in the morning when they arrived, but during lunch when a child asked what that thing on top of the wooden box was. I replied that I didn't know, that perhaps it was worth investigating further when I returned to class. At that moment, back in the classroom, the children realised that indeed this 'thing' was there. We then sat around and began to wonder what it could be. They started touching it and feeling that it was cold but somewhat soft. We took off the coloured plastic and realised it was clay, but they had never seen so much clay. We started to think about how we could work with Clay and everyone agreed that we could keep Clay on the box and everyone would then work there on the floor. In this context Clay was a bit of an anarchist symbol for me, in its own way it represented a collectivity, a community. Inside that block there were so many stories, so many individualities that had to emerge.

For the moment I will leave this experience in abeyance, I will take it up again in the next pages by analysing how I interpret and understand storytelling.

Stories and imagination matter

Some years ago, I was attending a course in psychology and in one of the lessons, the teacher turned on the projector without saying anything. A short movie of a couple of minutes was projected: two triangles were displayed and then a dot, after that, four lines that depicted a rectangle appeared, and one side of this rectangle opened and closed like a door. During these two minutes, the two triangles and the dot moved continuously, inside and outside the rectangle, touching each other, and so on. At the end of the film, the teacher asked us to write down on paper in ten minutes what we saw on the screen. After that, we had to read it in front of the class. It was interesting how every member of the class told a story and not simply a description like the one I wrote now. I don't remember my story, but I remember that I didn't see just geometrical figures when I watched that movie. This is an experiment performed by Heider-Simmel in 1944, and the first time it was proposed, out of 114 participants just 3 gave an "objective" description of what they saw, everyone else proposed a story as we did. What does the experiment tell us? According to Gottschall and following the idea of Simmel and Heider, this demonstrates how our mind could be defined as a storyteller mind. How our mind seeks continuously to engage with the circumstances through a story. As Gottschall puts it: "we are, as a species, addicted to story. Even when the body goes to sleep, the mind stays up all night, telling itself stories".[115] Moreover Gottschall underlines that:

> You might not realize it, but you are a creature of an imaginative realm called Neverland. Neverland is your home, and before you die, you will spend decades there. If you haven't noticed this before, don't despair: story is for a human as water is for a fish—all-encompassing and not quite palpable. While your body is always fixed at a particular point in space-time, your mind is always free to ramble in lands of make-believe.[116]

Stories surround us daily. When we deeply engage with a story, we don't sense the outside world, but we dig into the fictional world. A very simple example is when we read a book, if we are engaged in the reading, we don't notice for example how comfortable or uncomfortable the chair we sit on is, we don't notice the time passing and maybe someone must call us two or three times before we realise it. However, stories are our companions from the origin of our species.[117]

It has been noticed by Cometa[118], Gottschall[119], Boyd[120], Bruner[121], Niles[122] and others that we, as human beings, are immersed in a continuous narration. Gottschall defines human beings as *homo fictus, fictional human beings.* Cometa instead creates the concept of *biopoetic,* that is an intertwining between *bio,* in the sense of human beings' life, and *poetry* which is understood as narration. He uses the concept of *homo narrans* to underline once more the predisposition of our species to tell stories. Niles then elaborates a theory of narration using terms like "poetry," which stems from "poiesis" and refers to the act of creating stories, therefore narration. We could then assume that storytelling involves the act of both creation and gathering. However, it was Kurt Ranke in 1967 who introduced the term of *homo narrans,* in an article where he connects his thought to the work of Johan Huizinga *Homo Ludens,* arguing that humans are not only playful beings, but they are storytelling beings too. In the article *Problems of categories in folk prose* Ranke states that the human being needs stories to pass on culture, telling stories like playing is a fundamental trait of our species.[123]

Further, stories also help us to relate to the world, we could think about children's pretend plays, or how they help us in our capacity for cooperation. For literary Darwinists, these are evolutionary benefits for our species.[124] Stories were born as an oral tradition, but later stories also acquired a representational tradition, we can think of rock arts such as the Lascaux caves in France or Altamira in Spain. We can think of the narrations we can admire on old monuments left to us by ancient culture. Also, when entering a museum, for example, it is possible to see a figurative narration on the walls through all the paintings. And so on. Nowadays we are bombed by images and narrations through tv series or on social media. And we should not forget the literary tradition that with the introduction of writing has further expanded the possibility of telling and collecting stories over the centuries.

It is also important to consider the creative side of stories, especially those narrated orally, which offers the possibility to develop the imagination of both, the narrator and the listener. When telling or listening to a story, we can imagine a different world. My world is different from yours. It doesn't matter if you are the listener or the narrator. The narrator takes the listener on a journey, but s/he leaves the imaginative work to the latter.

Boyd, Carroll and Gottschall have a similar insight when they argue that stories help us live our lives. By studying different present and past cultures they suggest that it is ascertained how the arts collaborate deeply in the normal development of childhood and human beings.[125] Moreover, they argue that stories connect individuals with their culture and help people orient themselves emotionally, morally and conceptually.[126] They also underline that stories and the act of storytelling help individuals and groups in their development, in their cohesion, where social and emotional experiences are rooted in the group. Boyd suggests that art, and I would add storytelling, acts as a playground for the mind.[127] Gottschall believes that: "the free play of art, in all its forms, does the same sort of work for our mental muscles that rough-and-tumble play does for our physical muscles".[128]

What I would like to emphasize here is the understanding that stories can help us connect with the world and build a sense of community. Gottschall can therefore argue that stories also help to nurture our social skills.[129] It is correct to assume that not only children are users of stories, we adults also enjoy stories. However, as a parent and an educator, I have noticed how adults feel uncomfortable when it comes to the world of children, especially when it comes to stories. When children, for example, have their moment of pretend play, being it at school or at home but even in a playground, adults are not always able to tune into children's narrative moment, in the best case scenario adults are just "guests" in the story. Storytelling can be seen as an invitation to embrace a sense of abandonment, as a way to reconnect with our inner child, and to engage with and share stories with the children of today. To be a child is not something *less* than to be an adult.[130] It is just different, it is like two different cultures that meet and make the road together, by w/o/a/ndering.

With this background I tried to engage in a portray about the importance of storytelling for our human culture and how storytelling is an ontology of the human being. Thus, the importance in educational setting of spaces where children's stories can emerge. When I and my colleagues decided to use Clay as an invitation of a practice in the making, of w/o/a/ndering, we were already thinking that we would probably encounter stories. In a way, handing Clay over to the children (and why not, to us adults too) is like Simmel's film, you almost certainly get a glimpse of a story. Children are no different, they take one piece of clay at a time and start modelling creatures, houses, and everything they need in order to play a story. At the beginning of this experience every child created something for him or herself, with an internal story they tell themselves, and as the artefacts multiplied, children began to create stories that intertwined with each other... a house needed inhabitants... who wants to go? A rocket without a pilot cannot fly... then Mr Troll shows up and is interested in buying the rocket to fly to a new planet...

oh, wait... someone has a planet? And more... but has the elf ever ridden a water-spitting dragon?

Clay gave the opportunity to collaborate, discuss, think, imagine, and it offered the possibility to create new worlds and possibilities. Probably Clay is the best concrete material that has embedded storytelling, w/o/a/ndering and anarchism. My colleague and I rolled up our sleeves and began to participate in their w/o/a/ndering with clay. The block of clay was left there for weeks (every now and then we would add a bit of clay when it got too small or too dry), and there was no specific time of the day to approach Clay... our friend was always there. Hearing stories in a constant flow was something we admittedly hoped for, because through stories, even those told informally, new educational opportunities could arise, perhaps questions to ponder on. Through this experience I then appreciate what Pacini-Ketchabaw highlights on how educators can see materials "as movements, as encounters, as assemblages, as ecologies, as times".[131]

In conclusion, the aim of this part was to bring out the importance of stories from a social and evolutionary point of view. I touched on some arguments supported by literary Darwinism's scholars, like Cometa, Gottschall, Boyd, Carroll, and Dutton, who try to demonstrate the connection between biology, evolution, and stories. However, my intent was to broaden the gaze on the condition of the human being, that of the storyteller. A storyteller who is a creator and as such, s/he is also a collector of fragments of reality and imagination to which s/he gives a new life so as to create a common space with others, a space of belonging.

Storytelling: a practice that can foster empathy

As an educator I often found myself comforting crying children who had disagreements with their classmates, attempting to assist them in resolving their distress. In these situations, I used to and still say: "What if...? Can you tell me? What do you feel?", a very simple way of encouraging critical thinking and empathy.[132] These simple words can often make a big difference. Perhaps it is precisely this ability embedded in storytelling, the ability to identify with someone else, that has led me to use it as much as I could in my work. Maxine Greene's insights are interesting and their relevance for storytelling is valuable.

Greene observes that reproducing the way things are is not enough.[133] One reason is that in this case, we forget the plurality in which we are as humans. I understand this plurality not only as multiple relationships between humans but *within* humans themselves. Humans have their plurality within themselves, built upon experiences. That is why it is important to remember in the encounter with the other that we are part of a whole but equally everyone has their own experience.

Storytelling fosters imagination which allows us to educate to empathy, as Greene points out: "It is what enables us to cross the empty spaces between ourselves and those we teachers have called other over the years".[134] Empathy derives from the Ancient Greek *empátheia,* which means *inside the suffering or feelings.* This term was used by the ancient Greeks during theatrical performances to indicate the emotional relationship of participation that bound the poet to the audience. It is in this way that I also use biographies, to stimulate empathy, a book-experience should provoke questions, it should put ourselves in other shoes, it should make us think "what if…" or "in the spirit of…". Moreover, anarchism at work, implies to foster empathy. It is proper to say that my understanding of imagination is a social imagination a concept suggested by Greene as well.[135]

The relationship with the other is at the center of this thesis. The relationship between the educator and the educatee, and the relationship between the reader of this thesis and the scholars here displayed. In this educational reframing, the idea of "what if…" is a concept that we educators should always try to keep in mind. "What if" is an imaginative, problematizing, creative exercise. In this case, as I explained earlier, educators and children have the possibility to develop an empathic imagination. This approach leads to hypothesis, opens the door to a new world of possibilities. It could perhaps be understood as a problematizing imaginative practice.

As educators we have the responsibility to preserve a space where stories are the glue, or the ground, of a community made of storytellers. However, it is important to emphasize that the community cannot be decided and built a priori, this according to anarchist perspective too, or as Greene argues: through edicts or in a *rational* way.[136] The community should be built step by step, through a mutual appreciation of the builders of the community itself, educatees and educators, "in pursuit of themselves and it is to be hoped of possibilities for themselves".[137] However, speaking about community, I would underline that it is impossible to predict which kind of common world may be in the making. As educators, we can just give the best possibilities, options, and overall warmth to the member of such community, where "belief in justice and freedom and respect, inclusion for everyone are the principles not negotiable to foster a community of equals".[138] For this reason, imagination should always foster empathy, because as Freire underlines empathy makes dialogue possible, and if there is a dialogue there is the possibility to build a community.[139]

An example in this regard is an experience I had when I worked with a group of children on Shaun Tan's story *The Lost Thing*.[140] Through a shared story, we had the opportunity to reflect about ourselves as the boy does in the story. When we are not understood or listened to, we often imagine what we can do to listen and understand others. Furthermore, one of the peculiarities of each of Tan's worlds is the presence of strange beings, with shapes of all kinds. This gives the opportunity to children and adults to w/o/a/nder, and then create new worlds that arise from imagination. By this I mean that the extravagant shapes of the characters in Tan's world allow us to express ourselves as we are, everyone is welcomed. When we worked with *The lost thing*, a world was created, a community, where each child and educator could also share fears, fantasies, and this happened through the characters we had crafted. Inside the classroom a space in which we build a world that developed throughout the school year was recovered. A world that wanted to be a representation of our idea of community, a world where we were all equal. An equality based on the concept of empathy, of thinking about others. For this reason, I often use Tan's work, because he creates imaginary and visionary worlds where everything is possible.

Another moment I would like to point out was the project "Discovering with clay" which I had started with my colleague and that I am gradually unrolling in these pages. When I listen to the children's stories, I not only note them down in my logbook, always with their consent of course, but I also intervene in the story, perhaps by asking questions or perhaps by interacting directly with them. In fact, I always try to interact with them, otherwise I feel just like I am stealing, albeit with their permission, something from them. Children share their stories, and I think it is a sign of respect to share stories with them. Only in this way can I think of creating a horizontal relationship and not a colonising one. Anyway, back to Clay. At that point we left the classroom and started to explore our area: the parks, the forest, the square and other public places. We had provided some small boxes where the children could put clay inside and then carry it to the places we visited. Once at these places, we would mould something and maybe take it back to school or maybe leave it there. On one of our trips, on the way back, a child asked me why there were some people who often sat alone on the park benches. In fact there were several people, mostly elderly, who went to the park perhaps to feed the pigeons, the ducks, or just to see some people around.

From that observation, we started a mini-project where we modelled small creatures, which we would then leave in our city explorations to people who, in the sensibility of children, would appreciate a bit of company. We then also took this project to the nearby old people's home and the neighbourhood library and left them with our friends in the hope of creating new relationships. For me and my colleagues it was a very important moment because the children had shown themselves to be attentive to those around them. They also brought this back to school, as they were more attentive to their classmates who perhaps played more often on their own or were perhaps excluded from other games.

An approach to storytelling

While there are certainly intersections between storytelling and education, they also maintain distinct identities. However, enhancing these points of contact in educational practice would be beneficial. It has been displayed how human beings are immersed in stories, twenty-four hours a day, seven days a week. It is an essential part of humans' life, as it is education. Every story heard or told has some truth. "Each story illuminates' things differently, helping us to understand through the representations that narration offers us".[141] Human beings are the "product" of a narrative offered to or welcomed from others. Stories are questions, to which we should also seek answers, or following the examples of authors like Kohan or Ingold we should instead remain in these questions. These aspects are pedagogical. Demetrio argues that "Every moment of life is potentially a source of education we can make it the subject of our stories".[142] I strongly believe, like Demetrio, Greene and Ingold, that educational work should be built on creative strategies and solicitations, where storytelling, listening, and emotions can express themselves to the best of their ability.[143]

It is proper to underline that not every narration is educational, to be so it should leave something, a trace of itself in the one who tells and in the one who listens. It should produce a movement, a mutation beneficial to our well-being.[144] Once again, we can look at Tan's story *The Lost Thing*. Through this story it has been possible to speak about feelings, to better understand what other may feel, to enhance empathy. These actions produced a movement, and at the end of our w/o/a/ndering we were different. Through this storytelling, we rekindled our relationship with the world.

Ingold argues that telling a story is the ability to exchange experiences.[145] Thus, we can think to the practice of storytelling, where children and educators tell each other stories and also exchange their experiences, cultural experiences. My culture is different from that of a child. By culture, in this case, I mean the experiences that are made during life. The fantasy characters I encountered in my childhood are probably different from those of the children I met as an educator in preschool. Even between the children in the same classroom there are differences, some watch cartoons, read books or play games at home differently from other peers. When we tell a story then we bring to light our different experiences, which are shared within the community.

Jo-Ann Archibald argues that storytellers have a responsibility towards others, because of the power of stories.[146] In narration, we have the possibility to educate. I here understand *to educate* not only as a way to help the child to find his or her voice or individuality, but also to take care of him or her, to take care of the circumstances we are in. Demetrio enlightens us suggesting that "every story tells us something about us, talks about problems that are also ours".[147] In other words stories help us not only to question our practices, but help us to tune with others, for example, to empathic education. If we do not open ourselves to the other, the risk is to create an authoritarian narrative, where only one voice is heard.[148] This is also the premise of educational anarchism: an openness to others, through equality, mutual aid and collaboration and this would mean that we share our individuality within a community.

I am interested in Demetrio's understanding of education. He states that education is not always predictable, which I think works very well with anarchist principles and with Mortari as well as Zambrano's proposals.[149] Unquestionably as educators we have a desirable horizon to reach, like the w/o/a/nderer of Friedrich. To reach this horizon it is necessary to be aware of every circumstance we encounter on the way, every narrative moment, and transform this w/o/a/nder into pedagogical experiences. Demetrio encourages us to think about education as a "solicitation to think to creativity, to free solitary discovery. To think that we learn through trial and error, in a bumpy path that forces us to always start over".[150] However, Demetrio continues, we should think about education not only as an act here and now, rather we should think of it as a possibility to look at the past, at our missed opportunities, so to recognize our mistakes as educators. This switch from present-future to present-past is unusual, since we see education as a projection into the future. An education that is seen as a future horizon does not allow us to commit mistakes, as the future, in theory, should be "spotless", since we have "time" to plan it. The future should be better than the present. However, an education that allows educators to look back, to understand the mistakes, and to see the good we did as educators, helps us to be better educators. This then will be transformed in a better practice that looks at the future educational horizon.

Therefore, as Biffi argues, it is important to create suitable conditions to favor storytelling, to develop that innate competence that we carry with us.[151] I can also relate to what Armitage says, anarchist educators need to create the condition for education to occur.[152] I believe that in a community, especially if we want to approach it from the perspective of anarchism, we are *all* called to an educational practice. I mean that children can educate each other, and they can also educate the grown-ups. As I suggested a few paragraphs above, to educate is not only to lead, but also to care for the other.

It is important to foresee the possibility of w/o/a/ndering with stories outside the classroom too. When we went out and about the neighborhood with the children, we had educational moments where we learnt about life outside school. Sometimes I feel that school has become a place isolated from its context. Sometimes. I think it is important to keep this possibility of w/o/a/ndering alive inside but especially outside the school. Since if school is supposed to 'prepare' children for life outside, for adult life, it is also fair to let them participate in this social life. Clay, in its continuous transformation, accompanied us around the streets, through the forest, into the homes of the children. This continuous transformation was like a becoming, and to remain in question, like Kohan or Ingold encourage us to do. It means that one doesn't seek an answer, but another question, another possibility, another reflection to move forward. Another aspect we were interested in, was to invite parents, grandparents, to be part of this long collective story. When children brought home their artefacts, the parents had the opportunity to be engaged in this creative process. A collective story that was exhibited in the neighborhood library at the end of the year, to underline once more the importance of the whole community.

Storytelling and w/o/andering as pedagogical narration

In this final part of the chapter, I will focus on a very important tool that we have as educators in preschools. It would be better to say "we could have" since it is not a widespread practice. In any case, *pedagogical documentation,* which was named by the educators of Reggio Emilia, is widespread in both contexts in which I worked, the Italian and the Swedish one. Pedagogical documentation is an important tool to delve into a proper reflection on the pedagogical practice. However, I prefer to borrow the term *pedagogical narration* from Veronica Pacini-Ketchabaw. I would rather use Pacini-Ketchabaw's definition since I understand pedagogical documentation as a narration of a journey that children and educators accomplish together.[153] Biffi also suggests a "pedagogical narration, capable of weaving and containing other languages without losing its own".[154] In fact, quite often, speaking with other educators I see the tendency to treat pedagogical documentation as "simple documentation", collecting a certain amount of data, writing, taking photos, drawings, making videos, etc. They are preserved and then, eventually, shown to the children or parents to remember what has been done. Like the more and more common use of social media where the daily practice is exposed, but then not really reflected. In doing so we, educators, as well as children, lose the awareness of our complexity as human beings.[155] This complexity could be understood through the one hundred languages that children have, according to Malaguzzi.[156] Pacini-Ketchabaw gives this definition:

> Pedagogical documentation takes time. We think of it in terms of the Slow Food movement as compared to a fast-food approach. Significant amounts of time are required to document the children's learning, and more time is needed to study and engage with the documentation.[157].

However, this time is disappearing, and the pedagogical documentation, as stated above, is losing its depth, becoming more superficial, and oversimplified,[158] it could be understood through Ritzer insights as a pedagogical "McDonaldization".[159] This of course cannot work when we "embrace multiple perspectives and subjectivities, complexifying practice in ways that would be limited within a modernist discourse of objectivity and neutrality".[160] For this reason, we should do a step back and recover the gentle time mentioned in the introduction, a slow tempo where the encounter between educators and children becomes reflective and practical. Where circumstances meet and create new meanings.

It is possible then to appreciate how a pedagogical narration comes from the relationships that educators and children build in their practice, how a pedagogical narration is a political act, and the respect that everyone involved in the process of the narration has towards others. Moreover, how a pedagogical narration is a collective work, a collaboration.[161]

In this regard, my *praxis* as an educator moved from fast to slow. At the beginning of my career, I was told that we had to show our daily practice to the parents and outside the school. This meant for us as educators to "produce" every day an amount of documentation to display on walls or social media, to show what we did, and how we were "good" at it. This was done in order to have more visibility and possible future *clients*. The stress that this created was a factor that brought me to reflect on what we were doing, where were the children in all of this? Yes, they were present in the pictures, through their artefacts, and sometimes in their explanation to the parents. But it seemed to me that their voice was silenced somehow, like someone who speaks behind a glass, you can hear a distorted voice but not their *real* voice. For example, as educators we often reflect on documentation, we decide what to display and what not, autonomously without the help of the children, who are sometimes involved in a second reflection. In other words, the basic work is done by the educators, and any refinements is done in groups.

The more I acquired experience, the more I was convinced that there was another way to act, to be more here-and-now with children, and to foster a more anarchist practice through the pedagogical narration. The first step was to show clearly to the children when I was documenting something, to have their active contribution, if they wanted to add something or if they didn't want to be part of this narration, they could tell me. The second was to encourage children to make their own narration, and documentation, using a tape recorder, cameras, artefacts, or coming to us to narrate their thoughts.[162] The third was to collect all the records, put them on the floor of the room, and together, educators and children discussed and analyzed the documents, moving forward or staying on some educational moments, on some circumstances.[163]

When a project, a narration, was concluded we displayed it on the walls, giving a small book of it to the children, as a memory. It could take one month, two months or more. For us, the educators, it was more important to display a complete and reflective narration, that gave meaning to our practice, rather than to show social media crumbs. We were happy, and for us it was enough, when children on the way back home told to parents what they did at school, this was also a way to document, it was a recognition of our practice, children and educator. Further, a pedagogical narration, if done properly, fosters the possibility of an anarchist pocket since the praxis of the pedagogical narration is "not to know the child, but to participate with the child in making meaning, to live alongside children".[164] Moreover, I find this line from Pacini-Ketchabaw quite interesting, as she argues that "educators seek to make visible the strengths and competence of the child in the present, beyond preparing the child to be ready for the future".[165] This could be understood as an anarchist practice, and a disruption of neoliberal discourses as well.[166]

In our meetings with Clay, we encouraged children to document what they were doing. To do this they could take photos, draw pictures, record their voices or ask us to write something down. Each child had a small book with detachable sheets to document their w/o/a/ndering, and our idea was to collect all their documentation in one book that could then be printed in several copies and thus share this collective experience. This was obviously time-consuming for us, often even outside normal working hours, but it was always worth it. If I invite, as an educator, the child to actively contribute to his or her narration, keeping his or her voice heard and documented, where we give the meaning to the educational journey together, then I would consider this practice close to educational anarchism.

It is important to understand that when we reflect on our practice, as educators and children, it is not only to find practical solutions in the daily practice but "to use theoretical tools to reimagine new worlds and create new openings".[167] Pedagogical narration could help us reinvent our practice and be critical about it, "collaboratively reflecting with others is a key part of our leaning".[168] Pacini-Ketchabaw underlines there is a tendency to think of early childhood practice "as a simple matter that can be easily prescribed and directly applied".[169] This is what I aim in the various chapters of this dissertation, to show that it is not possible to prescribe education, and this is what Mortari, Zambrano and educational anarchism stand for.

Pedagogical narration is also a form of storytelling, it could be individual or collective. Children have the possibility to tell a story, the story of their journeys, their own discoveries. However, this story could also be shared with other children, and in this case, it is also interesting to see what children take with them about their experiences, to see if they create a common culture, a common place, a shared experience. Sometimes it happened that some child didn't feel to belong to that narration, they could feel left out. In that case it is important as an educator to understand why, and to prevent such situations, and in this case Ingold could argue that what we need is an attentive education. In addition, pedagogical narration could be understood under the concept of w/o/a/ndering, educators and children wonder and wander about their practice, their being with the world in the world. Their circumstances interact to give meaning to their encounters.

I would also suggest to interpret pedagogical narration like the attempt that Maria Zambrano does in her book *Filosofia e Poesia*, where she combines philosophy and poetry, and for this account storytelling.[170] According to Zambrano at the beginning philosophy and poetry were intertwined, then a separation occurred, philosophy became more and more important, and poetry lost its place, losing its importance. Pedagogical narration in a sense is the possibility to combine stories and philosophy, a philosophy understood as w/o/a/ndering, since we can document our wonder and wander, and this brings us through a transformative act.

As it has been said in the previous chapter, Zambrano's philosophical work is permeated with poetry, her work could be called poetic philosophy or philosophical poetry. When I think of pedagogical narration, documenting the stories that fill the air daily, whether it is the play children create during the day, or it is some creative activity in the atelier, my thoughts go to this poetic philosophy proposed by Zambrano and her existentialist philosophy that explores the human condition. By interweaving Zambrano's work with the practice of pedagogical narration, my understanding of it certainly becomes more philosophical.

I, finally, recollect an interesting suggestion of Ingold which is proposed in his text *Anthropology and/as Education* that is related to the work that educators and children do through pedagogical narration. Ingold affirms that

> the classroom is a place where much of the real anthropological work is carried on, a site of creative transformation in which we join with the thinking of our predecessors in order to go further, beyond what they would ever have imagined.[171]

This is the role of an educator (and I believe the educator is a bit of an anthropologist too), s/he should prepare a space for such transformative leading life.[172] Both the educator and the anthropologist in their work collect stories and tell and reflect on them. The central point, however, of Ingold's proposal, is that education should be seen not so much as an act of transmission rather as an act of attention. In this sense this is what I propose both in general educational terms, i.e. the educator must be attentive, both with pedagogical narration and storytelling. Attention, Ingold notes, is derived from *ad-tendere*, a Latin word that means to stretch towards something. In fact, when we are attentive, we have the ear stretching towards a dialogue, we have the eye catching an important moment, the hand picking up something, a step towards something that attracts us, and in this way, we can relate to the world. An attentive education is an education that is exposed to the world, that welcomes it, it is a transformative education. An educational practice that is intertwined with the anarchic educational idea and especially the act of w/o/a/ndering. Storytelling is a moment, in a perhaps formal educational context such as school, that can accommodate this type of attentional education.

In this chapter, through several theorists, I have given an account of storytelling and pedagogical narration, their contribution as educational spaces and as philosophical dimensions. The aim was to give the possibility to rethink this space, this *gentle time,* this anarchist-pocket. In the next chapter I explain my understanding of anarchism within education.

Notes

115 Gottschall, Jonathan. *The Storytelling Animal: how Stories Make us Human.* (New York: Mariner Books, 2013), p.8.

116 Gottschall 2013, p.9.

117 Cometa 2017; Illich 1994.

118 Cometa 2017.

119 Gottschall 2013.

120 Boyd 2009.

121 Bruner 1992, 2003.

122 Niles, John. *Homo Narrans, The Poetics and Anthropology of Oral Literature.* Philadelphia: UoP Press, 1999.

123 Ranke, Kurt. *Problems of Categories in Folk Prose.* (1967), accessed through https://it.scribd.com/document/465720749/Homo-narrans-Ranke

124 Dutton, 2010; Cometa 2017; Smorti, 1994.

125 Boyd, Brian and Carroll, Joseph and Gottschall, Jonathan (ed.). *Evolution, Literature, and Film: a Reader.* New York: Columbia University Press, 2010.

126 Boyd, Carroll, Gottschall, 2010.

127 Boyd 2009.

128 Gottschall 2013, p.30.

129 Gottschall 2013.

130 Korczak, Janusz. *Il Diritto del Bambino al Rispetto.* (Milano: Lumi Editore, 2014).

131 Pacini-Ketchabaw, Veronica. *Encounters with Materials in Early Childhood Education.* (New York: Routledge, 2017), p.1.

132 Mortari 2006; Greene 2000.

133 Greene, Maxine. *Releasing the Imagination: Essays on Education, the Arts, and Social Change.* (Jossey-Bass Publishers: San Francisco, 2000).

134 Greene 2000, p.3.

135 Lake 2013.

136 Greene 2000.

137 Greene 2000, p.41.

138 Greene 2000, p.43.

139 Freire, Paulo. *Pedagogia dell'Autonomia.* (Torino: Gruppo Abele, 2014c).

140 More about this in the chapter seven.

141 Demetrio, Duccio. *Educare è Narrare.* (Milano: Mimesis Edizioni, 2012), p.11.

142 Demetrio 2012, p.13.

143 Demetrio 2012, Greene 2000, Ingold 2018.

144 Demetrio 2012, Biffi 2012.

145 Ingold 2007, 2008, 2015.

146 Archibald, Jo-Ann. *Indigenous Storywork.* (Vancouver: UBC press, 2008), p.27.

147 Demetrio 2012, p.45.

148 Demetrio 2012.

149 Demetrio, Duccio. *L'Educazione non è Finita.* (Milano: Cortina, 2009).

150 Demetrio 2012, p.52.

151 Biffi, Elisabetta. Narrazione e Pratiche Educative: fra Infanzia e Adolescenza. In *Educare è Narrare.* Demetrio, Duccio (ed). 73–113. (Milano: Mimesis edizioni, 2012).

152 Armitage, Marc. Playwork the Anarchist Wing of Sociology. In *Education, Childhood and Anarchism. Talking Colin Ward.* Catherine Burke and Ken Jones (ed.),113–123. (New York: Routledge, 2014).

153 Pacini-Ketchabaw, Veronica et al. *Journeys, Reconceptualizing ECP through Pedagogical narration.* (Toronto: UTP, 2015).

[154] Biffi 2012, p.111.
[155] Pacini-Ketchabaw 2015.
[156] Malaguzzi 2016.
[157] Pacini-Ketchabaw 2015, p.121.
[158] Pacini-Ketchabaw 2015, Biffi 2012
[159] Ritzer, George. *The McDonalidisation of Society.* (Thousand Oaks: Pine Forge press, 1993).
[160] Pacini-Ketchabaw 2015, p.124.
[161] Biffi 2012; Confalonieri and Scaratti 2000; Smorti, 1994.
[162] Mattia 2011.
[163] Mattia 2011; Biffi 2012.
[164] Pacini-Ketchabaw 2015, p.15.
[165] Pacini-Ketchabaw 2015, p.xiv. See also Confalonieri and Scaratti 2000.
[166] Pacini-Ketchabaw 2015.
[167] Pacini-Ketchabaw 2015, p.33.
[168] Pacini-Ketchabaw 2015, p.19.
[169] Pacini-Ketchabaw 2015, p.xii.
[170] Zambrano, Maria. *Filosofia e Poesia.* (Bologna: Pendragon, 1998).
[171] Ingold, Tim. *Anthropology and/as education.* (New York: Routledge, 2018), p.8.
[172] See also Armitage, 2014.

Anarchism is the ideal that may never be realized,
just as the horizon line is never reached,
anarchism is the method of life and struggle
and must be practised today and always by anarchists,
within the limits of possibilities,
which vary according to times and circumstances.
Errico Malatesta

Anarchism aims to develop free and critical minds,
and in pursuit of this, cultivate the values of
liberty, equality and solidarity.
Petr Kropotkin

One step at a time is all it takes to get you there.
Emily Dickinson

CHAPTER FIVE

Towards an anarchist philosophy of education

What is anarchism?

It is not easy to give a linear, univocal answer and it cannot be otherwise.

In the attempt to answer this question, I found myself writing and rewriting this chapter several times. The risk of being misunderstood is just around the corner. As it is the risk of being labelled naive or utopian. Also, this chapter includes the concept of w/o/a/ndering as a compass, since I understand the educator within anarchism as a w/o/a/nderer. First, I will give a very brief history of anarchism, and some of its peculiarities. Then I will engage in a fictive dialogue with the British anarchist Colin Ward, and his contribution to the childhood discourse. I want to do this to show that despite its "controversial reputation", anarchism in some forms is commonly practised by most of us in different forms and moments. Further, I invite to read these ideas and concepts with an open mind but overall to think that everything I suggest in these pages is often an addition rather than a subtraction. An example is Paulo Freire, who despite his different background, is an important figure in the anarchist discourse within education, like Colin Ward stated himself.

So, what does anarchism mean? And what is its aim? To answer these questions, let's start from its symbol: the famous A surrounded by a circle representing the letter O. It comes from the motto that the anarchist Pierre-Joseph Proudhon coined "Anarchy is Order". Further, he said that "for genuine anarchists, anarchism is not a decadent lifestyle for malcontents or an anti-social creed, but a sincere social philosophy".[173] Anarchism, or better to say anarchy, come from the Greek word ἀναρχία (anarchia), ἀν means *without* and ἀρχός, *power* or *command* and therefore: without a ruler. The aim of anarchism is to establish a stateless society, where decisions are taken in a bottom-up direction, or it would be correct to affirm that anarchism aims to have a horizontal relationship between people.[174] In this understanding of relationships between the different actors of a society, political power gets closer to people and is held within the communities. In this regard it is understandable why anarchism is different from liberalism and Marxism, in the first case the social dimension is missed in order to have an individualist society, in the second the power is still in the hands of the few, creating a vertical relationship up-botton.[175] There are some practical examples of anarchist societies related to anarchist principles, like the Kurdish community in Rojava or the practice of direct democracy present in Switzerland, the small community in Spain called Marinaleda or in the past the Commune of Paris at the end of the 19th century. Many more could be mentioned here. Anarchists' communities nowadays are scattered everywhere, from the mountains of Italy to the plateau of Missouri. We could, for example, mention the attempt to create an anarchist republic in Catalunya, Spain, during the 30s of the 20th century. In this very occasion anarchists fought against both fascists and communists, and this shows the differences between communism and anarchism, at least at that time.[176] The aim of anarchism is to equally redistribute power within a community. In this dissertation the intention is to broaden the discussion about educational perspectives in relation to early childhood education and anarchism. It is worth to underline that there are several forms of anarchism, and the one I look at is social anarchism.

Structuring anarchism

Anarchism has a very long history which can be traced back to the writings of the British philosopher and journalist William Goodwin, between the end of the 18th century and the beginning of the 19th century.[177] The anarchist theoretical framework is a mosaic that has gone through different historical-cultural processes. Enlightenment, romanticism, positivism, evolutionism, neo-Kantianism, liberalism, and socialism are all projects and theories that have contributed to the evolution of anarchism.[178] Maybe it is for this reason that sometimes anarchism appear to be shaded and it could be related to several philosophical-political disciplines. Despite its lengthy history, anarchism doesn't receive as much attention and representation in academic circles as Marxism does; it is often viewed as the lesser-known counterpart.[179] Graeber notices, for instance, how Marxism has several scholars who named their own philosophical path, so we have Gramscians, Leninists, Althusserians, and many more. Instead, all the philosophical schools within anarchism take their name after a practice, like anarcho-syndacalists, cooperativists, individualists, and so on. "Anarchists like to distinguish themselves by what they do, and how they organize themselves to go about doing it".[180] Graeber sums it up in this way, "Marxism tends to have a theoretical discourse about revolutionary strategy, while anarchism focuses on an ethical discourse about revolutionary practice".[181] It is in this crucial difference that I see why Bakunin and Marx fell apart when they discussed their different ideas on society, and even if an anarchist should be open to a political pluralism, it is wrong to consider Anarchism as the little cousin of Marxism.[182] In other words, from a theoretical point of view, in anarchist thought there is nothing comparable to the critique of political economy, which is instead the heart of Marx's thought. According to anarchist thought, the radical critique of existing society is above all anthropological, ethical and political.

It is then important to say that anarchism assumes a reference horizon (anarchy), a tomorrow from which it draws its criteria for acting today, not only in the social body and cultural dynamics, but also in pedagogical practice. Anarchy and anarchism are not equivalent terms: they are inseparably linked, certainly, but they are not the same thing. Anarchy constitutes the ideal horizon; it is what to strive for. Anarchism is a historical action; it is both an individual and collective movement that acts teleologically (from tèlos) towards its horizon: anarchy. In other words, anarchism is that complex historical dynamism (social, political, cultural, pedagogical, etc.) that acts *here and now* in view of a not-yet-dislocated human and social elsewhere.[183] Beware: the anarchy we are talking about here is by no means to be understood as a concrete and defined model of society, it is not an *object* ready-made on a theoretical level that one would have to drop into historical reality.[184] It is a society in *becoming*.

For this reason, it is not easy to grasp what anarchy is, and why anarchism can take different forms. Thus, anarchism could be seen as a "demosaicization" as Marshall points out and this makes anarchism interesting.[185] One perspective highlights the divergent theories within anarchism's evolution, while another emphasizes the unifying thread binding these diverse ideological currents. As the Italian scholar Pietro Berti explains in the introduction to the book *La Buona Educazione:*

> There is an underlying inspiring principle, given by the irrepressible dialectic of freedom-equality-diversity. This principle holds together all these determinations, giving them a different meaning than any other pedagogical approach.[186]

Generally speaking, a pedagogy based on anarchism is activated when it is inserted in a framework that includes an incessant criticism of the principle of authority, therefore the ethical formation of the human being. Hence Berti implies that every anarchist theory is always a *pedagogical reflection*.[187] Therefore it is not easy to give a coherent picture of anarchism precisely because all theorists have experienced anarchism in different ways and anarchism is always in movement, it is ever-changing. However, the pedagogical reflection that anarchism invites us to do is not easily found in the philosophy of education's literature.

In *Anarchism and Education: A Philosophical Perspective,* Judith Suissa states that the absence of anarchism in philosophical texts and in the history of educational ideas stems from a difficulty in distinguishing between anarchism, libertarianism, and Marxist ideologies, as they often intersect within the realm of education.[188] Even if anarchism has its own way to see the world. Suissa also states, "The typical response of contemporary scholars to the anarchist idea – that it is 'utopian', *impractical* or over-optimistic regarding human nature".[189] Essentially, anarchy is the hypothesis of a human society freed from its alienated expressions and returned to itself, a society in which each individual can experience maximum freedom and self-expression, while taking into account the fact that each of the other individuals must also be guaranteed the same existential fullness. In anarchy, human beings are all equal in dignity and have the right to be recognized. So they must be able to enjoy the same social condition of possibility, but they are all different in the way each pursues their existential fullness. Maximum civil equality coincides with maximum existential diversity.

In fact, when speaking of an anarchic society, it must be remembered that in it, as in any society, individuals live in relation to one another, so the actions of each must necessarily take into account those of everyone else, of all those within whom, in the course of his or her life, the individual comes into contact. It is precisely here that the theoretical space for the pedagogical aspect opens up. In a hypothetical anarchist society, what forms should relationships with the other have? Pedagogical practice cannot therefore set itself the goal of eliminating multiple social conflicts by eliminating the conflicts between human beings, a goal that is clearly impossible. It is therefore a matter of educating not only in collaboration and solidarity, but also in managing conflict. To educate, therefore, is first and foremost to educate to understand ourselves and the reasons that move us, and to wish to understand the reasons that move others. Thus, to act on the conflict that opposes us in order to reduce it as much as possible, to give as much space to encounter and not to clash with the others. Striving to meet and recognise each other is essential to increase the social space of reciprocity, but so is being able to recognise the times, ways and reasons for non-recognition and possible conflict. To summarise: it is not the perfect life that we must seek, but a life in which as much space as possible is given to the path towards a more desirable arrangement than the existing one.

Further, McLaughlin speaks about *genuine anarchism*, and he refers to the practical idea to live accordingly to anarchist ideals, and as it will be illustrated later through Colin Ward's works, an idea of everyday anarchism.[190] That means small but practical actions in daily life, for example, cooperating with someone in need. I underline this because the risk is to understand McLaughlin as he intends that there is a *true* anarchist practice, drawn from some instructions or so, while there is not, but there is a practice grounded on some principles: freedom, equality, solidarity.[191]

With this in mind, we shall go back to the theory of educational anarchism. Education is an important pillar within the Marxist and more in general Critical Theory philosophical discourse. Education within Anarchism, instead, has not had such a relevant theoretical position. This does not mean that it has not been taken into consideration, in fact, even if we lack a theoretical corpus, we have important educational practices. It has been shown that between the 19th and 20th centuries, there have been several attempts to ground schools based on anarchist and liberal principles. The Spanish anarchist Francisco Ferrer y Guardia founded La Escuela Moderna in Catalunya, where in the early thirties of the 20th century they attempted to establish an anarchist society. The work of Ferrer y Guardia was then exported to the United States where several schools opened, and they are still running today. Paul Robin (1837–1912) started in France a school known as Cempuis. Lev Tolstoj in 1859 established Jasnaja Polyana, a school for the children of the farmers and the outcast of society, one of his ideas was that the only method of education is in the experimentation and the only pedagogical criteria is freedom.[192]

I here underline that every school mentioned is mostly for school-aged children from 6 years old and up. In my search, I have not really found any preschools. Trasatti points out that the Italian educator Maria Montessori in her reflections about children, childhood and adulthood developed some ideas like the care of children, the importance of the environment in the development of the child, or even when she criticizes the idea of the child as an empty vessel that must be filled by the adult, that could all be related to anarchist principles.[193] I believe that also the school of Reggio Emilia, in Italy, is based on some anarchist principles. For example, they originated after WWII and Malaguzzi, the founder, wanted a school that was independent from the State and the Church, a school that was done *with* the community.

Anyway, for this reason, for this vast anarchist universe, I choose to follow the work of Colin Ward, to use his anarchist horizon to foster the ideas of w/o/a/ndering, storytelling and anarchism itself.

Tomás Ibánez: thinking anarchy

Tomás Ibánez's work, *Anarchismo in Movimento*, delves into the intricate dynamics of anarchism, shedding light on its ever evolving and adaptable nature. The title itself, "Anarchism in motion," conveys the essence of anarchism as a dynamic, fluid force rather than a static ideology. Ibánez points out that the ontology of anarchism itself is to transform over time. If anarchism was immutable, it would not be anarchism.

Ibánez argues that the very ontology of anarchism demands constant change; an unchanging anarchism would contradict its fundamental principles. According to him, anarchism is not a fixed entity but rather a product of relationships within specific cultural, societal, and temporal contexts. This perspective aligns with the concept of w/o/a/ndering as I intend it, emphasizing the transformative potential of questioning and engaging with the status quo.

The diversity within anarchism becomes apparent as Ibánez highlights that anarchist ideas stem from practical experiences in various realities. While shared principles unite anarchists, their practices emerge from diverse contexts, resulting in a rich tapestry of thoughts and actions. Ibánez contends that anarchism thrives on a perpetual struggle against domination and would stagnate without this ongoing resistance.

A notable concept introduced by Ibánez is the idea of *extra-moenia anarchism*, encompassing practices not explicitly defined as anarchist but sharing themes, values, and references with anarchism. Movements like May '68, Occupy Wall Street, No Friday for Future, and the Seattle demonstrations exemplify this extra-moenia anarchism, demonstrating shared ideals through direct action and contestation of power.[194]

However, Ibánez redirects attention to everyday practices, emphasizing anarchism's role in weaving diverse social relations and fostering alternative ways of life. Anarchism, in Ibánezs view, extends beyond mere opposition; it actively creates different realities in the present. Ibánez suggests that anarchism is often unconsciously practiced, underscoring the need to recognize, defend, and sustain it.

In contrast to notions of a distant future transformation, Ibánez asserts that anarchism is a philosophy relevant to the present. Drawing on the idea that life is a continuous becoming that starts in the present, Ibánez views anarchism as a way of living, not just a way of making claims. The sought-after transformation may be partial and localized, manifesting itself as 'islands of freedom' within society, where educators can cultivate conditions for w/o/a/ndering and anarchist practice.

Ibánez acknowledges anarchism as a challenge to capitalism new public management and liberal systems. Anarchism's commitment to social justice and freedom among equals disrupts the foundations of competition, individualism, and control on which society is built. This disruptive nature, according to Ibánez, contributes to the resurgence of anarchism, aligning it with societal changes in recent decades.

The circular movement connecting anarchism to contemporary changes becomes pivotal in understanding its renewed momentum. Ibánez notes that thinkers like Deleuze, Foucault, Rancière, Butler, and Haraway, though not directly linked to anarchism, are appreciated in anarchist circles due to a resonance between their ideas and the evolving nature of anarchism. Despite the emergence of post-anarchism, Ibánez emphasizes the existence of room for neo-anarchism – a reinterpretation of anarchist practices in society.[195]

While recognizing the benefits of labels, Ibánez argues against the necessity of creating new ones. He contends that historical periods provide sufficient orientation without additional categorization. Ibánez's exploration encourages a nuanced understanding of anarchism, urging individuals to engage with its evolving nature, recognizing its everyday manifestations, and in doing so it actively contributes to its ongoing transformation within society.

Seeking a common ground

Anarchism, in its short and bigger understanding of society, has a distrust in the role of the State, and continuously criticizes the relationships of power.[196] However in these pages I will look at its contribution within education, and how it is possible to find distrust towards the educational system, where national curriculum are criticized as well as the neo-liberal approach to education.[197] A constant criticism of the vertical educator-educatee relationship, seeking to find a paradigm based on a horizontal relationship, which can be achieved in educational practice by considering and implementing certain concepts that formed the bases of anarchism. We have then talked about how anarchism is wide and not easy to map. In my readings something has emerged as a constant, and I am talking about mainly three concepts: freedom, equality and solidarity. Besides the idea of a stateless society, in the anarchist literature, these values are the most quoted and as an educator, I also find such concepts in the literature on early childhood education. These concepts, moreover, help us frame anarchism within education.

Freedom and liberty, in the anarchist literature, are essentially interchangeable, nonetheless, this concept is also the most misunderstood, caricatured or oversimplified idea.[198] Freedom is necessary to cultivate human nature, "freedom is a necessary condition for the development of one's potentials[199]". It is not just a philosophical concept as Daniel Guèrin suggests, for anarchists it is "the vital concrete possibility for every human being to fully develop all the powers, capacities and talents with which nature had endowed them, and turn them to social account".[200] Freedom is not freedom if disconnected from the circumstances, it is not individualism. "Freedom is to be understood within a social context. It is conceived as part of the development of one's potential".[201] As Malatesta argued, anarchism means freedom for everybody, with the only limit of equal freedom for others.[202]

Equality is connected, in the anarchist view, to the rejection of social or institutional hierarchy and domination. Equality is not to be understood as an aim, as an attempt to "equalize" society, and "fix" it from capitalism, but it must be understood as an *a-priori* condition that sees every human being as equal from the beginning. As an educator, I convey with Berkman when he suggests that: equality isn't about everyone having the same; it's about everyone having the same opportunity. Genuine anarchist equality is about liberty, not uniformity. People have different needs and desires, just as they have different appetites. True equality lies in the opportunity for everyone to fulfill those needs and desires.[203] In other words, educators must create a condition in the educational practice where children can express themselves in one or more of their languages. This concept is reprised by Kohan when speaking about equality.[204]

Solidarity or mutual aid is a concept developed by the anarchist and scientist Petr Kropotkin who argued that mutual aid is a natural and important phenomenon in evolutionary biology and social development.[205] Solidarity is a natural dimension for human beings, to evolve and protect the species, to cooperate and seek free associations within the social context. As Mueller argues: The anarchist commitment to the principle of solidarity is rooted in the recognition that despite potential differences, structuring our interactions and society around cooperation instead of competition is achievable with present human capabilities. This shift is not only feasible but also essential for upholding the notion of *equal liberty for all*.[206]

Human nature according to the anarchist idea is often seen as an unreasonably high standard or even a naïve opinion of what human beings are capable of. However, anarchists consider human beings to be capable of violence and selfishness, but also to be able of kindness and altruism. To carry out the best of human beings, to cultivate kindness and altruism, it is important that the social context favours and fosters this attitude. Human nature is, in other words, also the ground for freedom, equality and solidarity.[207]

Mueller suggests that, according to anarchists, traits like compassion, independence, and a sense of solidarity must be cultivated through properly facilitating environments.[208] If a child is to grow to value cooperation and solidarity with others, then children must practice cooperation rather than institutionalized competition with other peers. If children are meant to learn to challenge received truths and think for themselves as adults, then they must, while young, learn through action that encourage them to practice individual inquiry and challenge authority.[209]

Anarchist educators should engage and cultivate children's awareness about values like solidarity, and social and political questions as well. Of course, this is a difficult task, since educators must avoid becoming dogmatic, as Kohan reminds us, otherwise, they become like the society they criticize.[210] In this sense, it is not wrong to overlap the anarchism instance of an educator who engages in social and political issues with Paulo Freire's belief that educators must teach or be example of social justice, with the idea of an equal dignity between educators and educatees as common ground.[211]

Being an *anarchist* without realizing it

My journey to *becoming* an *anarchist* has been backward, not forward. I mean that the process has been accidental. I have always felt a tendency to question power, especially when it acted without a clear justification. I have dreamt, and still dream of, an equal society. Overall, a school where everyone can flourish according to their own individuality.

As Chomsky says, authority according to anarchism has a burden of proof to bear and must demonstrate to be legitimate.[212] It is not important where this authority is, it could be inside a family, a school, or global economy, but it must prove itself to be legitimate. For example, if I am walking around with my three years old son, and he decides to cross the road suddenly, when I run and intervene to stop him from this risky action, I am acting with an authority that is legitimate since it prevents a dangerous situation. So, this is the burden of the one who holds authority, who must prove that this same authority is legitimate.

Of course, it is unthinkable that this authority must validate itself every minute of every day, but as Chomsky argues it must be ready to be challenged and show such legitimacy.[213] An education that is based on anarchism is an anti-authoritarian, pedagogical practice that does not have an individualistic connotation but aims at the formation of individuality whatever the human material available. Everyone must give what one can give, one must be put in a position to fulfil his or her full potential. *Individuality* over *individualism.* Educators for example must create a condition in their classroom where each one of the educatees can perform at their best. The final "product" is not important here, the process through which you arrive at that product matters instead. The best of all possible worlds is a world in which there is freedom of being different or freedom in the difference.[214]

The key point is that people should therefore put their abilities to good use with others, not at the expense of others. As it is not easy to achieve, this is precisely the difference between the anarchist ideal and the individual concrete experiments of anarchism. In the various historical experiences of educational and pedagogical forms that were inspired by anarchism in most cases, the common goal was to combine freedom with justice, solidarity, and mutual respect.[215] Anarchy, in a way, is a perfect world made up of imperfect individuals. No one can claim to have more human dignity than someone else, as everyone has the right to be respected as much as those around them.[216] This way of thought and actions brought me to understand myself as an *anarchist,* even if in our complex society this is not easy. However, there is a possibility to fulfil, even if partially, our anarchist spirit. Anarchism has helped me to give a perspective, and through it, I try to read also circumstances where I am in, to seek for potential moments of anarchism.

I understand my being an anarchist through Pier Carlo Masini words when he stated:

> From the very first time I approached anarchism, instead of the prophets, aesthetes and poets of anarchism, I always preferred the positive anarchists: those who know how to combine the principles of freedom with those of association and solidarity: which begin with the individual but arrive at society.[217]

Masini goes on to argue the importance of supporting one's own reasons but also being able to listen to those of the others, of observing not only the visible and certain face of problems, but also the invisible and controversial ones. But above all, Masini invites us to look beyond the boundaries of one's own ideological side, to discover perhaps an often-unconscious anarchism that should be used not as a yardstick to measure and perhaps condemn others, but as a lens to better read into oneself and into society.[218] This is my anarchism and therefore I see a strong connection with the concept of w/o/a/n-dering.

Towards an anarchist education inspired by Colin Ward

When I was a teenager and also a student at university, I have always contested the way of teaching. The idea to read given books, without the possibility to choose, or to have an opinion about them, brought me more than once to leave my studies. But every time it happened, I met a teacher who helped me to "cool" down, and even if partially, for a moment, for an exam, to find my voice, my true interest. This experience brought me to think about another possibility of schooling, to be more critical towards the system, probably my anarchism started growing right there. At the same time, the experience I had when I was a toddler and a child in a preschool in my hometown was a positive one, my interest in Early Childhood Education studies probably flourished there. I still remember when some years ago I went to visit the school with my daughter, that was one year old, and the teachers remembered me, after more than thirty years. They even took old books where photos of me and my fellow mates were gathered and preserved. That moment, done by memories, showed me that it is possible to make an educational practice with a close relationship between educators and educatees. This reflection brings me to the second part of the chapter, where I would like to discuss in more details the role of educators in an educational practice within anarchism.

To develop Colin Ward's thought, my praxis, and my view on anarchism, I decided to engage in a fictional dialogue between Ward and myself. The references used here are of two kinds, quotes from Ward himself or quotes from biographers that have written about him. In the next pages I turn my gaze on the work of Colin Ward (1924–2010), one of the most influential anarchist thinkers of the twentieth century. Ward was also a pioneer as he is often defined a social historian. The British anarchist left his studies at 15 and began working at an architectural firm. Eventually, he returned to school to complete his studies and continued to work as an architect until the 60s. In 1971 he became an education officer for the town and country planning association and continued his career as a columnist and writer. Ward's desire is to keep open "the channels between childhood, education, creativity and social change",[219] and he shares my same desire. Moreover, as Scott-Brown highlights, the strength of Ward's thought is the relationship between common experience and anarchist principles.[220] This relationship gives birth to new lived experiences, and these experiences in turn contribute to redefine anarchist ideas.[221]

Could we have a chat about anarchism, Colin?

The sun is shining, the wind moves the clouds quickly across the sky. As always, I am late, or rather I am on time but I don't have time for one last check. My guest is coming, my children are missing, as usual they are around the neighbourhood. Emma... Enea... where are you? I hear voices coming from outside, from the garden. It must be them, together with their friends who live in our little neighbourhood.

Emma calls me, "Dad, there is a gentleman here, not so young anymore, and he speaks a language I don't understand..."

I wonder who could it be, so I go out.

"Mr. Ward!" I exclaim.

"Hello and welcome!"

"Good afternoon! And please call me Colin!"

"All right, I'll try my best!"

"Thank you for the invitation".

"Well, thank you for accepting. Would you like something to drink or eat? I have prepared a rhubarb and apple pie, perhaps together with an espresso?"

"It sounds perfect, could I have a glass of water as well?"

"Of course! In the meanwhile, take a seat, I'll be back in a few minutes!"

Some moments pass, and finally, our conversation can begin.

Me: *I'm writing my PhD thesis, and one of the layers I use is anarchism. It has been a journey I began a long time ago, but it has also been a backward journey. I mean that I look at my practices as an educator in early childhood education, and I seek a path within anarchism. However, I'm very keen on critical theory and overall, the work of Paulo Freire, the first educator that opened my eyes with his life and work.*

Colin: Well, I think it is important that you open up the possibility of an anarchist understanding within education. I believe that to be open to other ideas is necessary if one wants to grow. Remember that anarchism is an open-ended outlook rather than a finite outcome.[222]

Me: I see, I think you are an anarchist who likes to look beyond the hedge, metaphorically speaking. This is the reason why I investigate your work. Another reason is that your work has a temporal proximity to our times. I like to look at old philosophers, Kierkegaard, for instance, is one of my favourites, or take ideas from educators or scholars who lived some time ago, but when I speak about anarchism, I need something closer to show how important anarchism is today. Anyway, as I said, I like your look over the hedge, it makes things simpler, and it is easier to avoid struggles. I have read for example that you have a pragmatic *idea of anarchism.*[223]

Colin: I suppose you are right. I think that an anarchist society is impossible to create, it would mean a revolution in the true sense of the word, with all the consequences of the case. However, I realize that there are also spaces within institutions to promote this form of relationship between people.

Me: So, I could say that you think that "anarchy is ordinary, everywhere and always in action".[224] In this sense, you promote a daily anarchism.

Colin: Yes, I believe so. I believe that, overall, in childhood, we can see a possibility to foster anarchism. And in several context, we can create a space for daily anarchism.

Me: This is what I understand about your anarchism. These observations of yours arise mainly from observing children and their relationship with/in the urban space. I understand that you have in mind a decolonization of childhood by the adult.

Colin: As you know I have been a city planner during the '60s and '70s, and I was interested in seeing how children relate to the space, to the city.

Me: Very interesting. Some years ago, there was a project in Italy where the municipality of Correggio created a neighbourhood planned by children and architects. Colin, you have always been very attentive to the condition of the child in the urban environment. We should also consider that your reflections came from a historical period when children were often in the streets, and the urban spaces were a common space to foster a sense of community. A dimension that nowadays we in the West have lost. For example, there is a chapter,

Play as an Anarchist parable, *in your book* Anarchy in Action[225], *where you rethink play as an anarchist practice. Just a note, this is also what I seek with my w/o/a/ndering, an understanding of the circumstance we leave in.*

Colin: *This w/o/a/ndering seems interesting, and I believe I have w/o/a/ndered myself. I think it is visible in my book* The child in the city. *Oh, yes about the play. I am so fascinated about this connection between play and anarchism. But tell me more, what do you think...*

Me: *Well, in this context, the work of the Dutch historian and anthropologist Johan Huizinga is relevant as he reflected on the sense of play in human nature. On a different note, it's interesting and tragic that Huizinga died in 1945 after three years as a prisoner of the Nazis, he was incarcerated because he believed in freedom and equality, two concepts that didn't match the totalitarian and oppressive vision of the Nazi Regime.*

In the seminal work Homo Ludens *Huizinga gives an overview of the importance of play for animals and overall human beings. Through play we collectively manifest our understanding of life and the world. Play is a tool in the construction of meaning.[226] Play does not necessarily convert into culture, yet culture has play in its origin. Huizinga also emphasises how play is a pre-social fact; it is something innate in us as human beings. By playing we also learn to be with the other, in the act of playing there is a beauty derived from the harmony and rhythm inherent in playing.[227] Of course, we see this in both children and adults, when we play we often pretend to be others, we are transformed, we can take other points of view, and children have the pretend-play practice. In the human being, play itself becomes an element of quest, both spiritual and cultural.[228]*

Colin: *Huizinga's thought is interesting. We can learn so much by looking at the children in their act of playing.*

Me: *I understand that your observations start from the playful activity and the relationships that are formed in the space of a playground. However, playgrounds can provide two different approaches towards play and relationships, depending on how playgrounds are conceived and made. A playground with well-defined structures, such as swings, slides and carousels, will lead to a more authoritarian space, where the risk is to lose the fantasy of the play itself, a space that you suggest "calls for no imaginative or constructive effort on the child's part and cannot be incorporated in any self-chose or reciprocal activity".[229] Instead, a playground where there are no structures or attractions* *already made, but materials that children can use to build their own stories, is a space where imagination, growth and relationship development never cease.*

Colin: *I think that a space created with this logic is a step in the direction of the decolonization of childhood. In fact, a classic playground is a construction made by adults for children, who can play only with what has been designed and foreseen by adults.*[230]

Me: *Once you wrote that you visited Emdrup, a playground in Copenhagen, grounded in the '50s, where children have the possibility to create their own environment. And you said that "the noise, screams, and fights found in dull playgrounds, are absent for the opportunities are so rich that the children do not need fight".*[231] *Let's think about it, as adults, isn't it true that we ourselves as children had more fun playing with material collected in the woods, in the street or found at home? Observing our children or the children we meet in our life, we often see how the "done and finished" toy attracts the child up to a certain point, then it is more fun to find and create toys and play with objects that can take a thousand different shapes*[232]. *Huizinga argued that play is a free act, and that commanded play is no longer a play, at best an enforced replication of play.*[233]

Colin: *I often suggest this when I see children play, something that we can see in our day-to-day lives. Children's play "far from being a speculative vision of a future society, it is a description of a mode of human organization, rooted in the experience of everyday life, which operates side by side with and in spite of the dominant trends of our society".*[234]

Me: *Would you like some more coffee or anything else?*

Colin: *Yes, please. Anyway, could you tell me more about your experiences as an educator and a father?*

Me: *Balancing between ideals, beliefs and daily practice is not exactly easy. I mean that as a father and educator I have my vision and my wishes, but sometimes I must face the reality that I am a human being and I make mistakes. Sometimes what I wish to do and how to practice education is different from what I thought. I try to learn from my mistakes, from confronting other parents or educators, reading, and reflecting. For example, when I bring my children to a playground, or when I was an educator at the preschool and I went with the children, I have or had this double thought, on one side what I believe is the right approach, on the other side to find a balance with what other adults* *expect would happen in that context. A playground is a complicated place with regards to relationships that may or may not be created, but as a shared place it's full of possibilities and inventiveness.*

Colin: *A playground could be seen as "a kind of parable of anarchy, a free society in miniature, with the same tensions and ever-changing harmonies, the same diversity and spontaneity, the same unforced growth of co-operation and release of individual qualities and communal sense, which lie dormant in a society whose dominant values are competition and acquisitiveness".[235]*

Me: *In these words, and observations, I also see a connection, a description of storytelling or a philosophy with children's practice where children and adults can meet on shared ground, where telling stories or philosophizing are told and listened to and re-told. A movement of construction, destruction, and growth as you, Colin, suggested about adventure playgrounds, a place where there is a constant storytelling. I would also like to highlight other aspects of your anarchism, your openness, for example.*

Colin: *As Burke and Jones pointed out, I am not interested in criticizing what already exists, namely the various government policies, but instead finding new spaces for thought and action.[236] It is possible to say that I envision anarchism not as a great revolution, rather as a micro-revolution, a day-to-day opportunity.[237]*

Me: *I believe that your approach supports two actions. One action is not to focus on criticism but to propose a practical, alternative solution to the current status quo. However, there is an implicit criticism of policies, since proposing another model implicitly criticizes the present model. As it is my intention with my thesis. The other action is the attempt to make this anarchist proposal as universal as possible. Freire said that his pedagogy should not be exported but should be reinvented, and the approach to anarchism that you propose is very close to Freire's idea to reinvent according to circumstances. I believe that this is a correct way of proposing different visions when taking inspiration from the theoretical and practical work of other educators.*

Colin: *Exactly. My writing is about the relationship between people and the environment they are in[238]. In all my years as an anarchist, journalist, and city planner, I have always been fascinated by this dichotomy between space and people, how the space, the circumstances that surround us, can mould relationships, can foster inner growth. How educators, it doesn't matter if parents, adults, or professionals, can give the best possibilities to everyone. In order to* *do this, we must always rethink our position as educators. It's a process of continuously becoming, and reinventing.*[239]

Me: *I agree. In this case, as an educator in early childhood education and care, I can think of the different schools or educational possibilities that exist in the different states. For this reason, I think that enhancing stories, maybe with a philosophical dialogue, through a playtime, a wander through a city or a wood, can give us the possibility of reinventing ourselves continuously. In this way we can then create islands of micro-revolutions or micro-politics.*[240] *Nowadays the governance policies of the school systems in the western society may have a common denominator, inscribed in neo-liberalism. New Public Management requires from one side a top-bottom decision making, on the other side to realise that the system standardises it, leaving little or no room for local peculiarities. So, for example, in a school there is little room for education with children, but everything is planned for the children. This is how I understand your idea of daily anarchism, which "sneaks" into the institutions and so it can be proposed and carried forward. This type of practice must also re-evaluate the relationship between childhood and adulthood. A relationship, as I mentioned, based on equality.*

Colin: *This is exactly what I mean with daily anarchism. I see many possibilities to do this, but it's not easy. The bureaucracy has invaded everyday life, like water a sponge, you can bring it out but there will always be water left in it.*[241]

Me: *Hart observes that despite the increasingly interests and policies in favour of a bigger participation of children in the communities, on several levels, in what is called civic engagement, referring to Flanagan and Faison, children are still the actors in curriculum and planning, but they are not the designers or initiators of play/education because it is the teacher who designs it. Children autonomously experiment with collaboration, through play and storytelling, they "develop their own rituals and rules and struggle to find ways to resolve conflicts".*[242] *Additionally, this way children will reproduce adult forms of governance and overall challenge them. It is always Hart who notices that this daily activity of learning social participation "is the foundation of civil society and more fertile ground for thinking about how to foster citizenship than a school or a city council".*[243]

Colin: *Of course, I agree with Hart, but what do you take with you from his reflections on my work?*

Me: *I understand that even if we see this tendency in children to regulate themselves, "we fail to induct them into a world of decision-making, perhaps just because as adults, we have delegated to others the habit of deciding".[244] Moreover, as Hart suggests, regarding the time and space children have, adults need to address the double hurdle of parents' beliefs in which they have to use children's free time for more programmed learning.[245] I can translate this idea into the practice of storytelling, a practice that doesn't need to be programmed, and at the same time, this doesn't mean that an unplanned activity is meaningless. Sorry, I am taking up a lot of space, but I need to do this in order to clarify my position. Anyway, I would like to go back for a moment to discuss playgrounds.*

Colin: *Don't worry, I understand, these are things that take time to sink in. What would you like to discuss?*

Me: *I would like to go a bit further in the role of the educator since this is also a point of my thesis. If children can do "better" without adults... what is our purpose as educators?*

Colin: *There is a sentence of Moore that I think could help you, according to Moore playworkers are the only "trustworthy, down-to-earth, adults on their side, ready to help imagine and carry out the most outrageous plans children can imagine".[246] However, educators have responsibilities to provide some sort of regulations as well, for example for what concerns the general safety of the group.*

Me: *Like for example in the Summerhill school, where children are not allowed to do certain kind of things, like climb up a roof?*

Colin: *Exactly. Regulations are made to protect children's basic health and safety. However, these regulations could reinforce lack of individual choice and maintain childhood oppression.[247] Hart says that adults shouldn't disappear from the educational environment, for example if a child is bullied an adult need to intervene. Adults should be seen as role models, but not as overseers, rather they should be there with the children.[248]*

Me: *So playworkers, given the nature of their role, can move in the space of these rules with greater flexibility, guaranteeing protection and at the same time freedom. A playworker should guarantee an environment that Nicholson defines as a space where "both the degree of inventiveness and creativity and the possibility of discovery are directly proportional to the number and kind of variables in it".[249] This is also why I like to work with clay, because it gives an* *infinite amount of variables, as well as natural material. Anyway, in other words: what does a playworker do according to you?*

Colin: *I suggest that educators should protect the freedom of children in their play against the constraints of their social-political context[250]. Educators or playworker are allies in children's play. And as Hart suggests educators should rethink their role, instead of doing things* for *children, educators should do things* with *children. It is the only solution to enhance a critical spirit and to foster a feeling of citizenship.[251] So, as educators, we have a big responsibility to provide the right condition for an engaging educational practice.*

Me: *Reading Armitage I have found a theme that recurs in your writings, Colin, you wrote that what people do is more important than the reason why they do it.[252] Armitage, in his experience as playworker and anarchist, envisages that playworkers should create a space where children have the possibility to play how and with what they want. Instead, often the spaces, the environments designed by adults are projected following the idea of what and how children could play, or even what educators think they should play.[253]*

Colin: *Yes, and I add that "children are not apprenticed but actual makers, natural builders and manipulators of their environments".[254]*

Me: *You have developed your work around this aspect, the belief that children's curiosity must be stimulated and not blocked. Is it correct to assume that in your scrutiny of urban landscapes, in looking for example at the relationship between environment, childhood and adults, you understood that childhood itself was always and always will be marginalized?*

Colin: *Yes, but by observing children, I'm increasingly convinced that childhood should not be idealized as something pure, fragile, and therefore manipulated by adults, but as a time to be taken seriously, respecting its vision and perspectives. I could quote Alexander Herzen when he says, "the purpose of a child is…to play, to enjoy itself, to be a child".[255]*

Me: *Well, Burke and Jones got inspired from your work and they put aside the ideas we have about childhood, and instead they suggest "following what children actually do when they play".[256] It's like to say that children are natural philosopher, and as Kohan, I think it's nonsense. As educators, we need to help them in this process of philosophizing, without taking their place in the dialogue. I think that I have already taken so much of your precious time Colin, so thank you for this chat.*

Colin: *It has been nice and refreshing. I hope you can keep your interest in anarchism.*

And that's it. The intention with this dialogue was to give an insight about how I understand anarchism on a daily basis. In the next part of the chapter, I engage with some further reflections about anarchism, and I portray some small examples of daily anarchism to better contextualize Ward's discourse.

Contextualizing playgrounds: an anarchist perspective

It is possible to understand the dialogue with Colin through the following account of what happens in the playground outside my window. However, this playground is no different from other playgrounds, it is no different from other moments of daily life where there is a space free from constrictions, rigid rules and where children can experiment their freedom. We as educators can create these moments at any time in our educational practices, as an educator myself I have always tried to create such spaces, inside and outside the school. My children play outdoor for several hours, it is the first thing they do when back from preschool, and overall, during weekends or school breaks. It is nice because there is a nice gang of children here. Now that they are older, there is more freedom to leave them free from the cumbersome presence of adults. A watchful eye, an attentive ear from us is always there, of course.

I display here two circumstances to clarify what I portrayed until now. Sometimes I sit in the garden, and sometimes at the table in the playground, which is a meeting point for children and their adventures in the middle of the house. I usually read or write, but a little piece of me is there with them to play. My interest in relationships has become more interested, more attentive, especially since I have more consciously embraced anarchism, or at least its intention. For example, sometimes it is evident who is the leader of the group and who instead follows. There is no real horizontal organisation, at least not explicit and not self-forming. However, the leader, if one can call it so, is accepted, as it is self-justifying[257]. It happens that there are struggles to become the leader, if they do not agree, the group splits in small groups, sometimes even groups made up of a single child. But the interesting thing is that they collaborate and, probably without realizing it, continue to play together. In short, the idea of being together, and playing together, is stronger than the idea of being in charge.

The group tries to find its own balance. Anyway, these dynamics become much more fragile in the active presence of an adult as if the mere presence of the adult create a state of judgement, of oppression, of dependency. Indeed, observing this adult-child relationship, I also noticed how it changes in relation with the adult. I mean an adult who is present, like me when I work in the park, or who puts himself "inside" the play, like the children, does not disturb as much the group's relationships. On the other hand, an adult who actively observes from the outside, but without participating, yet intervening from time to time in moments of discussion, like a "peacemaker", becomes like the gears in a clock full of sand. The gears stop working, and so does the group of children.

Another interesting episode happened when I was an educator at a pre-school several years ago. In this preschool, where I stayed at the beginning as an observer for a month or so (I did an observation for my studies), and then worked there for some extra months, there was a peculiarity: there were no toys. At least what we, as adults, consider toys. Educators provided fabrics of various colours and shapes, pillows, and some wooden sticks (in addition to the material in the atelier for art activities). Children could collect and bring to school natural objects collected on field trips into the wood. This reminds me of Colin's experience at Emdrup playground in Copenhagen.

Anyway, there was a democratic educational project and although other educators did not openly state it, it was an anarchic one. They had been inspired by some principles present in Huizinga's Homo Ludens, and under-stood play as a free activity in which the individual takes part according to his or her own choice. Huizinga further argues that play goes beyond mere physical existence, it becomes an element of spiritual and cultural research[258]. I would say that there are also elements here that can be traced back to anarchism, the idea of a choice to participate, a choice, as it was then explained by the edu-cators, that allowed the children to build the rules of play together. It was probably an extra-moenia anarchism.

The idea of not having actual toys was done mainly for three reasons. To cultivate imagination, to lower the level of conflict, and to be more sustainable. The educators were aware that the world outside was different, there were play and conflicts, yet the educational idea was also to give a different view of the world, an alternative horizon. In this framework, the partnership with the parents was very important, because they were the link between the preschool and the world.

Reading this triangle made of parents, educators and children in retrospect, I found it was very close to the idea of cooperation, equality, and community in anarchism. In the triangle, everyone was involved equally, and the coopera-tion between parents and educators, parents and children and children and educators was evident. This meant a functioning educational community was being built. I feel that this experience was close to Ward's observation about children and playgrounds, where a good adventure playground is in a continual process of destruction and growth.[259]

Adulthood and childhood within anarchism

Speaking of Ward's thoughts, I have highlighted his observations on the relationship between adulthood, childhood and the environment. Certainly, his observations arise from his idea of social anarchism, where, in the broad sense of the term it includes the economic, social and political aspects of daily life. Thus, anarchists scholars suggest that people can base a relationship on cooperation without imposing structures of domination.[260] Furthermore, another important aspect of his thinking is also highlighted, an active citizenship as a necessary component in education, "whose ultimate goal is to create critical and creative social actors".[261] Ward gave great importance to the environment and even Malaguzzi defined it as the third educator.[262] A proper environment, so classrooms, playgrounds, and more, should enrich the educational experience of the child, and the educator together with the child should try to create a proper space.

It is the relationship and balance between adulthood, childhood and the environment that allows for a meaningful educational path. These three subjects, adults, children and the environment, can relate to each other through play. Play, is a fundamental part of children's lives, but at the same time, it could be a place of dominion for adults. It thus becomes a place of resistance for children. As Ward said, play could be presented as pockets of disorder. Playtime is an important moment for the children, in this pocket children can experiment a sense of hope and optimism[263], it opens many possibilities of relationship and fulfilment.

This allows us to understand how children are interdependent and autonomous in the complex web of relationships with others, and environments. Play allows us to understand also that the world is not closed and fixed, but we have the possibility to reinvent it. "Children through play commit a subversive act, they can re-imagine everything in a way that adults can't".[264] Thus, play could be seen as a microcosm of a free society. I see play as storytelling, a space of collective experimentation in which for the time of the encounter, things can be held together and reworked.

We as adults must recognize children as co-researchers. If we recognize this, it is possible then to set out Ward's vision about education which celebrate autonomy, mutuality and engaged citizenship. And, as Ward once said, he did not aim to a city as a childhood city, he envisioned a city where children live in the same world as he did.[265] Also because even if adults control the space, or think to control the spaces, children find their own way of finding forms of dissents.[266]

To clarify, I draw from Malaguzzi[267] and Rinaldi[268] the idea that children are co-researchers, which means children construct their knowledge, and educators are not only co-researcher with them, so in a spirit of equality, but they must provide spaces, physical spaces and spaces of trust, so relational, spaces of dialogue, where children can express themselves, freely.

In the previous pages, I have given a broad look at anarchism, its origins, and its contradictions, looking at what can be defined as the core of anarchist ideals[269], such as fraternity, equality, mutual aid, and human nature. Anarchism is undoubtedly a political philosophy, and I understand anarchism using the concept of w/o/a/ndering and using what Marshall claims, namely that anarchism is fundamentally existentialist[270], as an ontological perspective. Existentialism and anarchism emerge from different philosophical traditions; however, they share some common themes. They emphasize individual freedom and autonomy, rejecting external constraints on human potential. They also criticize established power structures and encourage individuals to take responsibility for their actions and the world around them. Some scholars like Marshall have explored connections between existentialism and anarchism, noting overlaps in their criticism of authority and emphasis on individual agency.[271]

Anarchism is a fundamentally human way of being, which must be revitalized through example. Through w/o/a/ndering we can know, perceive and interpret the world. Through anarchism we can propose an alternative society, an awareness.

Anarchist education is consciously and essentially fallibilist and contiguous.[272] Fallibilist because it wants to educate to doubt first, doubts on education and educators and their methods. Then because it is aware that the error is an extraordinary self-educational resource.[273] Anarchist education does not foresee any final goal, no new human being is being built according to predetermined parameters. A practice that we as educators can enhanced in our daily educ-action.

Choosing Ward was also a way to moderate the idea of a stateless society. Indeed, not all anarchists believe in the State as an absolute enemy. There is no doubt that the State, in the past and present, is in too many cases the real root of frightening negativity for much of mankind. Yet, in the anarchist world there are more nuanced and articulate interpretations, which no longer regard the State as the absolute negative but re-evaluate it, at least partially, precisely from an anarchist perspective. Ward, for example, proposing pockets of anarchism, goes in this direction. Especially in a society as complex as ours, a form of State could be necessary, but these pockets of anarchism are also necessary to maintain a critical spirit. Transposing this question to the field of pedagogy, an educational theory inspired by anarchism must come to terms with the fact that it is surrounded by institutional pedagogy, with the State on its side. What is to be done, then? Perhaps, one can hold firm to anarchist inspirational criteria and at the same time realistically reckon the world around us, aiming to transfer as much of the anarchist 'quality' as possible into institutional pedagogy. In the same way, anarchists, while not abolishing the State, could show its limits and socially share their awareness of it. In this way, it will be possible to overcome the inadequacies of the State and the formation of a more evolved civic consciousness. It would be a step, however small, in the direction of anarchy.

In the next chapter I will reflect on education and educator's role through some scholars and educators who lived or live a philosophical-pedagogical life.

Notes

[173] McLaughlin, Paul. *Anarchism and Authority, a Philosophical Introduction to Classical Anarchism.* (New York: Routledge, 2007), p.11.

[174] Ibanez, Tomàs. *Anarchismo in Movimento.* (Milano: Eleuthèra, 2014).

[175] Ibanez 2014.

[176] Ibanez 2014; Marshall 2010.

[177] Marshall, Peter. *Demanding the Impossible, a History of Anarchism.* (Oakland: PM press, 2010). Ward, Colin. *Anarchism a Short Introduction.* (Oxford: Oxford UP, 2004).

[178] Marshall 2010; McLaughlin 2007.

[179] Graeber, David. *Fragments of an Anarchist Anthropology.* (Chicago: Prickly Paradigm, 2004).

[180] Graeber 2004, p.5.

[181] Graeber 2004, p.6.

[182] Graeber 2004.

[183] Marshall 2010; McLaughlin 2007; Chomsky 2013.

[184] Marshall 2010; McLaughlin 2007; Chomsky 2013.

[185] Marshall 2010.

[186] Berti, Pietro. Introduzione. In *La Buona Educazione.* 11–15. Codello, Francesco (ed.) (Roma: Franco Angeli, 2005), p.12.

[187] Berti 2005.

[188] Suissa, Judith. *Anarchism and Education a Philosophical Perspective.* (Oakland: PM press, 2010).

[189] Suissa 2010, p.13.

[190] McLaughlin 2007.

[191] McLaughlin 2007.

[192] Codello 2005.

[193] Trasatti 2014.

[194] Ibánez 2014.

[195] Ibánez 2014.

[196] In this case look at the works of Ibanez, 2014; May 2011; Chomsky 2013.

[197] Chomsky 2000; Codello 2015; Trasatti 2014.

[198] Mueller, Justin. Anarchism, the State and the Role of Education. In *Anarchist Pedagogies: Collective Actions, Theories, and Critical Reflections on Education.* Haworth, Robert H. (ed.), 14–31. (Oakland: PM press, 2012), p.17.

[199] Mueller 2012, p.17.

[200] Guerin, Daniel. *Anarchism: From Theory to Practice.* (New York: MRP, 1970), p.7.

[201] Mueller 2012, p.17.

[202] Malatesta, Errico. *Errico Malatesta: his life and ideas.* (London: Freedom Press, 1993).

[203] Berkman, Aleksandr. *What is Anarchism?* (Oakland: AK press, 2003), p.164.

[204] Kohan, Walter. *Paulo Freire: a Philosophical Biography.* (London: Bloomsbury, 2021).

[205] Suissa 2010.

[206] Mueller 2012, p.19.

[207] Suissa 2010; McLaughlin 2007.

[208] Mueller 2012.

[209] Mueller 2012.

[210] Kohan, Walter. *Philosophy and Childhood.* (New York: Palgrave, 2014).

[211] Freire 2014b; Freire 2018.

[212] Chomsky 2013.

[213] Chomsky 2013.

[214] Malatesta 1993; Kohan 2021; Burke and Jones 2014.

[215] Marshall 2010.

[216] Malatesta 1993.

[217] Masini, Pier Carlo. Prefazione in *A come anarchia o come Apua. Un anarchico a Carrara. Ugo Mazzucchelli.* Rosaria Bertolucci. (Carrara: Quaderni della FIAP, 1988), p.VI.

[218] Masini 1988.

[219] Burke, Catherine, & Jones, Ken. *Education, Childhood and Anarchism.* (New York: Routledge, 2014), p.xxv.

[220] Scott-Brown, Sophie. *Colin Ward and the Art of Everyday Anarchy.* (London: Routledge, 2023).

[221] Scott-Brown 2023. See also Ibanez 2014.

[222] Scott-Brown 2023, p.9.

[223] Scott-Brown 2023.

[224] Scott-Brown 2023, p.1.

[225] Ward, Colin. *Anarchy in Action.* (Oakland: PM press, 2018).

[226] Huizinga, Johan. *Homo Ludens.* (Kettering: Angelico press, 2016).

[227] Huizinga 2016.

[228] Huizinga 2016.

[229] Ward 2018, p.124.

[230] Ward 2018.

[231] Ward 2018, p.126.

[232] Nicholson 1972.

[233] Huizinga 2016.

[234] Ward 2018, p.18.

[235] Ward 2018, p.128.

[236] Burke and Jones 2014.

[237] Burke and Jones 2014.

[238] Wilbert, Chris and White, Damian F. *Autonomy, Solidarity, Possibility, the Colin Ward Reader.* (Oakland: AK press, 2011).

[239] Wilbert and White 2011.

[240] Ibanez 2014.

[241] Ward 2014, 2018.

[242] Hart, Roger. Children, Self-governance, and Citizenship. In *Education, Childhood and Anarchism. Talking Colin Ward.* Catherine Burke and Ken Jones (ed.), 123–138. (Ney York: Routledge, 2014).

[243] Hart 2014, p.126

[244] Ward 2018, p. 178.

[245] Hart 2014.

[246] Moore, Robin. Design for Urban Play as an Anarchist Parable. In *Education, Childhood and Anarchism. Talking Colin Ward.* Catherine Burke and Ken Jones (ed.), 139–156. (Ney York: Routledge, 2014), p.143.

[247] Ward 2018.

[248] Hart 2014.

[249] Nicholson 1972, p.5.

[250] Ward 2018.

[251] Hart 2014.

[252] Armitage, Marc. Playwork: the Anarchy Wing of Sociology. In *Education, Childhood and Anarchism. Talking Colin Ward.* Catherine Burke and Ken Jones (ed.), 113–123. (Ney York: Routledge, 2014), p.119.

[253] Armitage 2014.

[254] Burke and Jones 2014, p.xix.

[255] Herzen, Alexander. *From the Other Shore and the Russian People and Socialism.* (Oxford: Oxford University press, 1979), p.51.

[256] Burke and Jones 2014, p.xix.

[257] Ward 2018.

[258] Huizinga 2016.

[259] Ward 1978, 1995, 2018.

[260] Graeber and Wengrow, 2021.

[261] Breitbart, Myrna Marguilles. Inciting Desire, Ignoring Bounderies and Making Space. In *Education, Childhood and anarchism. Talking Colin Ward.* Catherine Burke and Ken Jones (ed.), 175–185. (New York: Routledge, 2014), p.176.

[262] Malaguzzi, Loris. *Loris Malaguzzi and the Schools of Reggio Emilia.* (New York: Routledge, 2016)

[263] Lester, Stuart. Play as Protest. Clandestine Moments of Disturbance and Hope. In *Education, Childhood and anarchism. Talking Colin Ward.* Catherine Burke and Ken Jones (ed.). (New York: Routledge, 2014).

[264] Lester 2014, p. 203.

[265] Ward, Colin. *The Child in the City.* (London: Architectural Press, 1978).

[266] Ward 1978.

[267] Malaguzzi 2016.

[268] Rinaldi, Carla. *In Dialogo con Reggio Emilia.* (Reggio Emilia: Reggio Children, 2009).

[269] Suissa 2010.

[270] Marshall 2010.

[271] Marshall 2010.

[272] Suissa 2010.

[273] Kohan 2021.

You cannot buy the revolution.
You cannot make the revolution.
You can only be the revolution.
It is in your spirit, or it is nowhere.
Ursula Le Guin

I rebel therefore we are.
Albert Camus

We walk, not in order to arrive at a promised land,
but because walking itself is the revolution.
John Holloway

CHAPTER SIX

Towards an *aionic* education

I am literally sitting under the stairs in what I call my lair and I feel like Harry Potter. My children are at preschool, and I can imagine what they are doing now. At the same time, I see them here at home, their presence is everywhere, even in my lair. There is my daughter's red car parked under the chair, I have lost count of the hours she has spent playing with it, one of the first toys she got and now it is Enea's turn to play with it. I think of the stories Emma told through that car, and now new stories await to be told by Enea. Some books by Beatrice Alemagna and Shaun Tan with beautiful images and stories lay on my desk, while drawings that my children hung on the wall in front of me, and some old photos too. In a sense, I am surrounded by stories. Then I think about my relationship with my children as a father, am I a good father? I can't really answer this question, but I will ask them one day.

This question leads me to think of myself as a child and then as an educator. I believe it is important to think about ourselves as a child, as Freire suggests in a letter to his niece Cristina.[274] This helps us to get closer to a time that has passed but it is still present in our lives when we encounter other children.

As a child, I always felt the urge to be free, to go my own way. As an educator and a father, I try to foster this. I mean that in my practice, in my relationship with others, like children or colleagues, I try to give them a space to feel free, to be free, to experiment possibilities. This is also the reason why I think anarchism is so appealing to me. This urge for *freedom* could be defined as an urge for *equality*. In this chapter and in this dissertation, I look at the equality that anarchism seeks, and I encourage us as educators to fight for it, not to take equality and freedom for granted, as anarchism urges us to think critically about it. I understand *equality* as an axiom, as Rancière suggests[275] and in this case, the idea of equality overlaps with the anarchist's one.

In this chapter, through the theories and practices of educators and scholars I try to give *one* understanding of education and of the relationship we adults have or could have with children. These authors are not anarchists, at least not that I am aware of, but they can contribute to the anarchist discourse according to the spirit of Ward anarchist pockets, or Ibanez's moving anarchism or extra-moenia anarchism.

Revolutionary education

According to the Cambridge dictionary, revolution means *a big change or improvement in the way that something works or looks on, in the way that people do a particular activity.*

In his book *El Maestro Inventor*, Walter Kohan underlines that education is inherently revolutionary. Put differently, true revolution cannot exist without education. Hence, education can only truly fuel revolution when every individual in society is educated. A society where education is not widespread cannot foster revolutionary change. Education must be accessible to all, or it loses its transformative power.[276]

Education and revolution are two concepts often related and the books on which this chapter is based on, just like others in this dissertation, present this relationship between revolution and education.

Simon Bolivar, who was a revolutionary in Latin America between 18th and the 19th centuries is still an icon with several murals dedicated to him in the whole continent. I am saying this to underline the relationship between revolution and education. Enlightenment fostered an intellectual revolution which then induced social and political revolutions like the ones that occurred in France, Italy, Latin America and North America, or like the industrial revolution which moved from the United Kingdom to the rest of the world. Anyway, I will not speak about armed revolutions, but intellectual or rather educational revolutions. Revolutions in education then arose time after time, we can think to the introduction of preschools during the 19th century, compulsory schools, universities that now are open to everyone (depending in which part of the world one lives, of course), internet, public libraries, and so on.

Further, another insight I read in Kohan's suggestion is the necessity to invert our priorities and social values. We need to rethink our position as educators in relation to our cultural context, as well as our experiences and our possibilities. We can accomplish our revolution in our practice. A revolution that in Kohan's words is presented *to invent the school,* or as Kohan writes in Spanish *hacer escuela,* which means *make the school.*[277] The revolution that Kohan proposes is a daily revolution, like the one Ward would like to see through the daily anarchism, those micro-revolutions that should occur in our educational spaces. With this understanding it is possible to observe here a connection with several other educational approaches, like Philosophy for Children, which aim to rethink the school as a space to foster critical thinking, cooperation, empathy, imagination on daily bases, and this is also how I understand storytelling.[278] A philosophical attitude and thought, before even being a pedagogical and educational one. Lorenzoni suggests retracing the words of Alberto Manzi who said that

> revolution is a perpetual challenge to the encrustations of habit, to the insolence of unchallenged authority, to the complacent idolisation of self and the myths imposed by the media. This is why revolution must be a normal event, a continuous renewal, a continuous thinking and doing, debating, and doing.[279]

I intertwine these words with what Ibanez argues in *Anarchia in Movimento*.[280] The act of a revolution involves a determination to dismantle the established structures of dominance. It is a deliberate endeavor to obstruct power in its various forms and an initiative to establish spaces that fundamentally deviate from the values of the prevailing system and the lifestyles influenced by capitalism.[281]

Ibanez argues that the emphasis on the present's radical transformation leads to efforts in creating living spaces that defy societal norms and generate rebellious subjectivities. However, it's now clear that past revolutionary ideals, promising societal hegemony, led to inevitable totalitarian tendencies, as often seen in those policies influenced by Marxism. Additionally, a universalism concealing the desire to erase differences, while claiming applicability to all, practically rejects legitimate political pluralism and values.[282] As an educator I agree with this idea of Ibanez. Maybe in its wholeness it is not easy to relate everything to the daily practice. Anyway, it is possible to "use" something, for example when Ibanez speaks about universalism. As educators we know that everyone is different, everyone has his or her own voice, so we need to foster activities where individuality comes out, as we have seen.[283]

I found a connection in this poem, the shortest in English literature, which says: "Me, We". It was uttered by Muhammad Ali, and I find the strength of these lines extraordinary. "Me, we" was a way of saying that we are all one, something unique, and that the actions of individuals affect everyone. Because this is the power of words: a few words are enough to say great things. We can't do a revolution alone; we can't even conceptualise equality if we are alone. This is the reason why I often write *we* as I feel part of a whole that is much bigger than me and my ideas. I write as an educator and yet as a father and an adult, so the meaning that I give to *we* is about being an educator with all its nuances.

If we give a look at the biologos of the authors displayed in this dissertation, we can appreciate how these educators have spent their lives *together* and *for* the other. As we will see in the flow of this chapter the acts and practices of some these authors were not taken for granted, their ideals asked for sacrifices and sometimes they paid with their lives. Their strength was to live a true philosophical life, where theory and thought flowed like a river into daily educational practice.[284] They have lived consequently to their ideals of equality and freedom towards every human being. Paraphrasing Kohan, I could say they *hacer educacion*.[285] To make education, as they *reinvent it*.

They made their revolutions. It is time that we carry out our revolution which does not mean sensational actions, a few small gestures are enough to make big changes. Compared to the great systemic revolutions, the daily educational practice, made up of small things, often and willingly leaves deeper marks in the educatees and in the educators. Each of these educators, although they dreamed big, dreamed of changing society, they made a virtue of necessity, and they changed their daily practice in order to give a different future to those who met their circumstances. For this reason, I look at anarchism as a daily practice, done in an anarchist pocket that could make the difference. Here I could provide a very simple example, I do not know the reader, but I have had some teachers that made the difference in my life, we should think of it this way. I will make a difference in the life of the ones I encounter. We cannot think to change the sea, we need to think to inspire the drops that form the sea. In this, I think of Franco Lorenzoni and his activity as a teacher in a small school in Umbria, Italy.[286] In his daily practice he reinvented himself and inspired dozens of teachers.

A w/o/a/ndering between present and past

Walter Kohan's *El Maestro Inventor* and Jacques Rancière's *The Ignorant Schoolmaster* have played significant roles in shaping my growth as an educator. Two very similar works in which both take the first step in their reflections about education from two educators who lived in the same historical period, between the 18th and 19th centuries. Kohan follows Simón Rodríguez, an educator who lived in Latin America, while Rancière is inspired by Joseph Jacotot, a French educator who fled in Belgium after the French Revolution. Both educators had in common a revolution in which they participated: Jacotot lived the French Revolution, while Rodríguez took part to the revolution that Simón Bolivar carried out in Latin America. Moreover, there are two similarities in their pedagogies. The first one is that both saw the other as equal, they th/f/ought for others, for the outcasts. The second one is that their educational practice and reflections arose from two inceptions that they had through an encounter. In these pages, thus, I try to relate their educational and philosophical experiences with the role of an educator in Early Childhood Education, and how they contribute to enrich anarchism.

Rodríguez, in his w/o/a/ndering, met an illiterate child whose name was Thomas. During play time, Thomas sparked a revelation to Simón. When a hat landed on a balcony, perplexed on how to retrieve it, Thomas ingeniously suggested using Simón's shoulders to climb up. This simple solution profoundly impacted Rodríguez's perspective on education. It raised the question of how an illiterate child could devise such a clever idea. The realization unfolded: intelligence is universal, but not everyone has equal opportunities to showcase, nurture, and develop it. This moment marked the beginning of Rodríguez's transformative journey.

Jacotot, instead, had another kind of epiphany, an epiphany with grown-ups. In Leuven, he began teaching at the university, but his students came from the Flemish part of Belgium, and they didn't speak the language of Voltaire and Descartes. At the same time, Jacotot didn't speak Flemish. They couldn't communicate with each other. Eventually, a book, *Telemachus*, came to the rescue. It was published in a double text French and Dutch and, through a translator, Jacotot gave instructions to his students who had to read, write, speak, and reflect about it, using the Dutch to learn the French. Step by step, week after week, they succeeded in speaking and writing French. At this moment Jacotot wondered: how was it possible that they learned to speak and write French without someone who explained the language? Rancière underlines that from that moment Jacotot understood and proposed the idea behind his practice which is *everyone is equal*.[287] We can relate our practice as educators in preschools to both these epiphanies, how many times a child surprised us with an intuition, a question, an observation? How often did we give them proper attention? I think that this is what sometimes you could do to foster an attentive educational practice.[288]

One thing that I find interesting is that neither Jacotot nor Rodríguez had a linear education growing up, they had their issues with authority and how education was given. In different ways both of them eventually found their way of making an education for themselves, they were just too curious about the world. They needed to find their way of learning things, questioning the surrounding world.[289] Rodríguez and Jacotot are perfect examples of w/o/-a/nderers.

Rodríguez and Jacotot considered the other a peer, and both concluded that every human being has the same intelligence, in particular Jacotot argued that the only difference between people is the strength of the *will* to learn.[290]

The teacher's role is to foster this *will,* to encourage and verify that students use this *will* to learn, question, and move forward in their w/o/a/ndering. Certainly, the concept of will can also be interpreted from an anarchist point of view, the possibility to express oneself, to achieve, to develop one's wishes. However, I find myself uneasy with the concept of will, as it now seems intertwined with a politics that promotes the fragmentation of society, placing sole responsibility on the individual. When listening to politicians discussing social welfare, such as unemployment benefits, there is often the rhetoric that if someone is jobless, it is because they lack the will to work. Consequently, they argue that withdrawing economic support will motivate individuals to find employment. This reductionist perspective implies that success or failure is solely a matter of willpower. Similarly, within the framework of new public management, where standardization reigns supreme, individual circumstances are often overlooked, and adherence to predetermined standards becomes the primary focus.

Considering this, I prefer to replace the notion of will with that of curiosity, a concept later endorsed by Paulo Freire.[291] As educators, our role is to foster and cultivate this inherent curiosity within children. Rather than emphasizing compliance with standardized norms, we should strive to create environments that encourage and nurture curiosity. It is through exploration and discovery driven by curiosity that learning and growth occur.

Following Jacotot, Rancière suggests that everyone, even the ignorant one, can teach what one doesn't know, since we must stimulate the *will* in the other.[292] Reframing Rancière's proposition through the lenses of Jacotot, we can substitute the ignorant with the child in Rancière's equation, emphasizing curiosity over will. This educational philosophy, introduced by Jacotot and embraced by Rancière, aligns with Rodriguez's and, as we will explore in the subsequent chapter, Freire's perspectives. It posits that educators can learn from those they educate. These educators advocate for active, critical listening, fostering openness to possibilities. Thus, I argue that curiosity, rather than mere will, is paramount. As educators, it's crucial not only to be curious about the world but even more about the other. A relationship grounded in curiosity can catalyze new avenues of w/o/a/ndering.

Rancière then asks: do we really need an explicator? According to him, we do not. We need an educator that challenges our *curiosity* (or *will* in Rancièrean terms). This observation is drawn from the self-questioning that Jacotot did in Leuven when he saw his students learning a foreign language without explanations. Rancière clarifies it by saying that "what stultifies the common people is not the lack of instruction, but the belief in the inferiority of their intelligence".[293] In this case I see a connection with the practice of education within the frame of anarchism, where the educators offer to the educatees the possibility to grow according to their interests. There is always the risk to be an explicator, not to let children experiment their way in learning, for example through play, or storytelling. As an educator I should prepare the space for their w/o/a/nder, and in their w/o/a/nder I can't be an explicator.

I would like to stress that it is important to think of educational practice as a *doing with* as opposed to a *doing for*. At the time I am writing this part, I have just finished a course as a teacher, where the students did a training period of a few weeks in some preschools. In the discussions I had with them before, during and after this experience, some interesting observations emerged, observations that took me back a few years to the time when I was working as an educator myself. So nuancing Rancière's concept displayed just a few lines above, I intertwine it with a criticism that emerged in the students' accounts. The preschools environments observed by the students are often pre-established by the teachers, with little possibility of transformation by the children, and above all the content of these spaces is often 'fixed', and the activities themselves are often steered by the teachers with little regard for the children's intentions. And even more so, curiosity is certainly not fostered in these activities. For example, it is often impossible to move and mix toys, or lay in different environments. Building blocks cannot be mixed with the farm animals, dolls cannot be used with toy cars, and so on. Photocopies with drawings to be coloured are offered instead of blank sheets to first draw and then colour. If a child asks me for a drawing of a horse, why give a photo-copied horse instead of trying to draw a horse together? Here in these small examples, I find a risk of stultification, where the child and the educator do not embrace a path of curiosity.

Moreover, Rancière endeavors to establish a theory underpinning equality among human beings, positing it as an inherent condition, *a-priori*, that is inherent to human existence. Thus, equality isn't a transition from one state to another but rather a fundamental aspect of being, it is a *state of being*. Consequently, in educational practice, the focus should not be on achieving equality as a final goal but on fostering its realization. Kohan emphasizes that every individual's life possesses inherent possibilities, rendering each life equally meaningful. No life inherently surpasses another, a principle applicable universally, whether within educational environments or beyond. A political education is founded on the belief in the intrinsic value of all lives and their potential to challenge both individual and societal norms.[294] In this perspective, it is the educatee who becomes the spring of the educational action.

Kohan underlines an important aspect of Rodríguez's transformative journey. In his w/o/a/ndering around Latin America Rodríguez, founded several schools. However, his work didn't last, he faced the opposition of the oligarchy.[295] Nevertheless, Rodríguez left a significant philosophical and educational legacy, and Kohan suggests that we should understand Rodríguez as an initiator.[296] Rodríguez's noteworthy life lies in his persistent efforts despite the challenges of establishing a school for everyone and facing constant opposition. Embracing risks, attempting and acting may result in failures, but they can also sow seeds that yield discoveries over time.[297] While standing still, obviously, is risk free. Rodríguez challenged the existing social order, advocating for the inherent equality and dignity of all individuals. He, embodying anarchist principles, not only theorized equality but exemplified it in his daily educational practice, serving as a living example of an anarchist educator who paves the way through action. His intention was to build a school that is useful for the growth of human beings and their freedom, as Kohan states: "This, Rodriguez's way, is a philosophical, pedagogical, political and existential alternative".[298]

According to Kohan, unfortunately, the same space (the school) that should accommodate the philosopher, the educator, and the craftsman of the soul, becomes a hostile place, which rejects them.[299] Kohan underlines how the scope and hope of Rodríguez is to change the paradigm of imitation in favor of a paradigm based on invention and thought. Inside the schools, we can find the most precious treasure: children. In fact, they are the protagonists or rather the individuals to whom governments, companies, and educators, must pay attention to. It is important to remember that childhood is here and now, it is not a future project.

From this portrait we can draw a vision of children as active, thinking actors, and they can reason on par with adults. If as educators we approach childhood this way, we can abolish hierarchical relationship, which are replicated in society, and in this way, we come closer to an anarchist approach to education. Adults must not be afraid of having an equal relationship with the idea of childhood. Indeed, through encounter with childhood, adults can find themselves. Precisely through children and their creative time, their play, adults can learn to become creative and w/o/a/nder again. The school should be a place of experimentation, inspiration and experience, and as well as life it is the best teacher for each of us.

> The teacher can inspire in one, and arouse in others, the desire to know. The teacher is the one who gives rise to the desire to know in order to understand and transform one's own life and that of others.[300]

Kohan portrays Rodríguez as one who loves to say *we invent, or we err.* The work of every teacher, of everyone who is concerned with education, is to invent school, inside (and outside) of schools.[301]

These philosophers challenge traditional views on education, they suggest a more inclusive and democratic approach to education. Rancière advocates for an equal intellectual capacity, however it is important to understand that everyone is also different, we can always remember the children's one hundred languages.[302] Kohan advocates for an educator that w/o/a/nders, open to the other, a creative and curious educator. In other words, autonomy and self-directed learning should be the ground of our educational practice. If we w/o/a/nder together with the children, the outcome is unpredictable, and it is possible to see this when we practice storytelling with children. The initial sparkle to the story is the same but we don't know where the story will go. As Kohan notices: "It is worth pointing out that equality is not opposed to difference, but rather, more precisely, to inequality. We can therefore all be both equal and different".[303] And anarchism grounds its ideals on this understanding of equality.

Walter Kohan's philosophy of education

I here portray Walter Kohan's understanding of childhood and his philosophy of education. His philosophical proposal helps us, as educators and adults, encounter the child as ontologically equal to us. The reason for this investigation is Kohan's ability to read between the lines, to see nuances that otherwise could pass unobserved.

Kohan's philosophy resonates deeply with the notion of exploration and interconnectedness. He perceives Freire as a *connective boy*, adept at weaving together diverse thoughts, experiences, and theories, akin to a spider spinning its web.[304] Similarly, Kohan employs this approach, intertwining various philosophical strands into his discourse. Furthermore, Kohan utilizes philosophy for children as a framework to engage in discussions about childhood and education, creating a space reminiscent of Ward's concept of *daily anarchism.*

In Kohan's work, it is always possible to feel a tension between practice and theory, between life and writing. In a certain sense, it is a philosophy that narrates life, a narrated life that is also philosophical practice. It is possible to appreciate this aspect in the philosophical narrative of his works like *El Maestro Inventor* or *Paulo Freire: a Philosophical Biography*.

Within the practice of philosophy *with* children, Kohan grounds his considerations about the relationship that we as adults and educators have towards childhood. In the choice between *for* and *with*, one can already understand the approach towards childhood. *For* stands for a practice thought somewhere else by someone else, and probably imposed. *With* stands for a practice fostered together, an encounter between childhood and adulthood. I prefer this definition because it implies, in my understanding, a more equal relationship with children, we do philosophize *together*. At the beginning of Philosophy for Children, the idea of Lipman was to create a method to help teachers and children to philosophize, so it was something already given. Lipman created a series of stories with questions at the end, to simplify the role of the teacher as facilitator. With time, this method became an approach where teachers and children can build up together their philosophical encounters.

According to Kohan there is a widespread understanding that children are *natural philosophers,* just because they ask questions.[305] Children can be philosophers, but it is not something automatic, and asking questions doesn't mean to be a philosopher. For this reason, Kohan criticizes the kind of idealism or romanticism towards childhood that we as adults have, overall, when we try to juxtapose childhood with philosophy, or when we consider children as natural philosophers.[306]

Kohan argues that the key to meaningful interactions with children involves letting go of preconceived ideas about them and childhood. It is emphasized that the abundance of knowledge accumulated in psychological sciences from the late 19th to the late 20th century has created a perception that everything about children can be anticipated, leaving little or no room for genuine surprises and encounters. This is seen as a significant challenge in our era.[307]

Moreover, Kohan wonders: what if there is someone who can anticipate what a child may think? Educators need to undress their prejudices and welcome others with their hi/story and walk together into life. I think that the key words are *attention* and *curiosity*.[308] We need to be attentive and curious towards children otherwise their thoughts cannot take shape, cannot become alive. This means that children cannot foster their individuality, but they lose themselves in the mass and maybe, only at that point, they will seek for individualism.

Furthermore, regarding the concept of thinking, Kohan argues that in the practice of philosophy for children a risk of dogmatism exists, since *to think* as a philosophical concept is not something easy to explicit. What does it mean? What do we do when we think? Kohan thinks that it constitutes a political act in the context defined by Jacques Rancière. He suggests that the value of thinking lies in its ability to unveil the previously unseen, revealing aspects of existence unbeknownst to us. Hence the educator's focus tends to be on the methodologies of thinking, contemplating how we think, and the various skills, techniques, and strategies involved. But as educators do we consider thinking as merely a technique or something more? In addition, as educators we should ponder if, in the act of thinking, we are employing skills or engaging in different processes, such as experimentation or meaningful encounters.[309]

It is not important which activity we organize with children, rather it is important to consider when we educate, since by doing it we are making a political act too. Educators don't need to *think too much* about theories or skills to undertake their *praxis*. The risk is to be a technician of education and as educators, we need instead to be open to the encounter, to the unknown and to make our reflections to implement our practice, here and now.[310]

Moreover, Kohan sees that one of the main strengths related to bringing philosophy to school consists in its being able to open our thoughts. According to him, through philosophical practice, we can think about what has not yet been thought of, to what seems unthinkable, we have the possibility to make an experience that is a kind of journey of the thought, without paths already mapped out.[311] It is in this way that I understand and approach storytelling in my practice. When we work within the practice of storytelling, aren't we going through a path that hasn't been mapped out yet? Aren't we making a journey of thoughts, an experience shared with others too?

It is not easy to use experience since it is a journey that develops along the way, we need to be attentive and reflective all the time, we need to listen carefully. We need to think about experience as a unique journey where, as I am doing in this thesis, we do not aim to give any answer that has to be followed step by step as in a handbook, but rather a map to orient ourselves. Kohan's words help explicit this concept better:

> I believe that educational experiences are always singular and, in a certain sense, unrepeatable, because they are inextricably linked to the context and to the subjects that intervene from time to time. So, I don't think it's interesting or even possible to transfer an experience to other contexts.[312]

Kohan is following the footsteps of other educators when he emphasizes the importance of saying, "do it *with* me" rather than "do it *like* me". Education is always a dialogical practice. So, if we place ourselves on par with the educatees, we are obliged in a way to cooperate with the other to look for the knowledge we miss, this way the teacher ignores the hierarchy in thinking.[313]

Certainly, Kohan asserts that equality constitutes a fundamental political concept, yet he suggests that a deliberate divergence in intellectual capacities, considered politically favorable, serves as a rationale for economic and social disparities.[314] Nevertheless, if intelligence were universally perceived as equal, it would necessitate a critical examination of the societal framework that perpetuates these inequities across its historical economic, social, and political dimensions. Delving deeper into the discourse on education, it becomes evident that intellectual variations are entrenched within our political fabric. On the one hand, conservative ideologies seek to justify these differences, whereas progressive ideologies endeavor to alleviate them. Nonetheless, both approaches inadvertently endorse social and political disparities. Thus, the dialectic of equality and diversity underpins the pedagogical process. An uncritical approach to education, characterized by mere memorization or deterministic causality, fails to foster genuine learning experiences. As Kohan contends, those who cling to such dogmatic principles are unlikely to inspire innovative thinking or meaningful progress.[315] Storytelling could be a space in which educators do not chase the idea of childhood as a future adult society and I would relate storytelling to Kohan's idea of time.

Kohan draws his understanding of time from Ancient Greek, where Greeks called *time* in three different ways: *Chronos, Kairos and Aion*.[316] The first is defined as chronological time, there is a before and an after, we can measure time through a clock or a calendar, but it only has past and future, it doesn't consider the present, because when it does, the present has already vanished into the past. The second is the time of opportunity, a qualitative marking of Chronos.[317] Kohan makes an example, where Chronos within education is the time that organizes, programs, controls and disciplines, while Kairos is the time of uniqueness, for example, where I can learn a specific matter in a given time. It introduces timing to school time. Aion, is the most interesting since it defines the present time. The here and now. It is the time to appreciate what one has at that moment, and this appreciation is a way to slow everything down. Considering educational practices through an anarchistic lens and incorporating the power of storytelling allows us to align our approach as educators with an aionic perspective, focusing on the present moment and context.

What I believe is relevant in Kohan's philosophy of education is this parallelism with anarchism, even if he doesn't mention it. But for example, when he says that "philosophy is a practice that problematizes dominant ideas, beliefs and values"[318] of course I run with my mind to what anarchism is. Moreover, it is his idea of a practical philosophy that I intertwine with anarchism, and with storytelling as well, and embedded in his discourse we can find the concept of equality among all those engaged in an educational practice and, widening the gaze, we could define it as an equality that is transversal within human beings.

Janusz Korczak

Some decades after the death of Simòn Rodríguez, Henryk Goldzmith was born in Poland in 1878. It seems almost as a handover from the educator of Caracas to the educator of Warsaw. As Rodríguez, also Goldzmith changed his name and became Janusz Korczak, but contrary to Rodríguez, he kept his new name until the end of his days.[319] A further commonality they shared was their passion for writing. I have not yet mentioned this, but Rodrìguez had a writing style that reminded of an oral approach, his writing was alive, and it had a voice and not only deep content. Korczak had a similar approach, maybe less oral but still close to people, yet being both literary and poetic.

If Korczak's childhood was a typical middle-class childhood, his adolescence was not. He attended the faculty of medicine and became a medical doctor, but his interest in education and childhood was vivid and he eventually left his profession as a doctor to become an educator. He started the House of the Child, Dom Sierot in Polish, which was an orphanage, but he refused to consider it as such. He wanted Dom Sierot to be a place of peace, freedom and where children could grow up as human being discovering their potential. Nowadays it seems obvious, but we must think about those times, where for example corporal punishment was accepted. Well, at Dom Sierot, it was not. In his life as an educator, Korczak put children well-being above his own. He spent endless hours solving each problem that Dom Sierot faced, even when they were obliged to move into the Warsaw Ghetto after the Nazi occupation. Within Dom Sierot's walls, a small city existed, we could define it as a little Polis, where everyone was treated as equal. For example, during the meetings to discuss something, Korczak and the other educators had the same right as every child to vote, I mean that Korczak's vote was not more important than a child's vote. There was some rule that couldn't be overruled, but they were rules about general safety, like don't climb on the roof. Inside this Polis there was a journal, written and printed by the children, everyone had a task and works to do, and so on. At Dom Sierot an important activity was the theatre, where children and educators were invited to participate as spectators but mostly as actors. For Korczak, theatre and stories were at the core of good educational practice to foster a growth into children and educators.

On the 8th of June 1942, Korczak and his children exposed and saluted with a ceremony the *Green Flag,* which was the symbol of Dom Sierot. Green as hope, green as nature. On the 18th of July, the children acted in a theatrical piece, *The Post Office* by Rabindranath Tagore, where the main character, a child, who is locked up in a room, is sick and dreams of running through the fields, and eventually dies. This piece was censured by Nazis and Korczak chose it because he thought it was necessary to speak and embrace death with serenity. And this theatrical piece was the last thing that Korczak did at Dom Sierot with his children. Four days later, Nazi troops began to deport the inhabitants of the ghetto to the concentration camps. Korczak was caught four times and for four times he was spared, due to his influence and status outside Poland too. However, since he didn't want to abandon the 200 children of Dom Sierot, he decided to walk together with them to the trains and board with them, four educators and the *Green Flag,* all the way to Treblinka, where he refused the last possibility to be freed, and followed the children to the gas chambers.[320]

I think that in this last action Korczak showed what it meant to be coherent, he lived until the last breath a philosophical life. Korczak showed to be *ontologically equal* in its highest expression, when notwithstanding the circumstances he stayed until his last breath with his children in Treblinka. Only a person who truly believes to be equal to others could decide to accept circumstances that would lead to death. Thus, Korczak did not only write about equality, but he also lived it.

In Korczak's book, *The Child's Right to Respect*[321], it is possible to notice how the concept of equality is connected to childhood and education. The book begins as so: "We lived with the idea that bigger is better".[322] It could be added that we still live with it, our society is based on it, on being bigger, faster, stronger, and newer.

Korczak argues against this idea, where small means banal, devoid of interest. "Little people, little needs, little joys, little sadnesses",[323] and with this line the first page of the book ends and I invite you to ask yourself if you have ever thought in such a way. I admit I did, and I still do. There is another fact, the adult must bend, kneel, to reach *down to* the child, in a physical and psychological effort. How often do we speak with children looking down on them? How often do we ask them to stand up, to rise to us instead of crouching down to them? In this way, Korczak tries to warn us that in doing so we risk replicating such behavior in children, they will learn that little is not a good thing, and it is better to be big. According to Korczak, we have a disrespectful disposition towards the child believing that he does not know anything, he has no idea what adult life is and its difficulties. The image that he gives us is that of an adult who sees children and childhood as a burden. This image becomes clearer when the adult, educator, or parent (it doesn't matter in Korczak's terms), begins to feel resentment towards the child. The point is that we hope that the child will follow us as we wish. We can be indulgent in some situations, and "accept" how he or she is, but he or she must give us something back, in terms of obedience and submission.[324] Korczak highlights the tendency to impose unquestioning reverence according age and experience rather than allowing individuals to exercise their own judgment.[325] Thanks to this thought, it is possible to *understand* the unbalanced relationship that we have with children, and that the concept of equality within the ontological dimension doesn't exist.

It is in the second part of the book where Korczak helps us resolve this unbalanced relationship, allowing us to see the child from another point of view. The child is an equal to us. We usually say that children will be our future in this sense, we collocate childhood in the future, in another time.

> The children did not fall from the sky by surprise, only to stay with us for a little while. Children constitute an important percentage of humanity, as inhabitants, our fellow citizens, our lifelong companions. They have been, are, will be.[326]

Korczak suggests looking at the child as a stranger in a stranger's land; who is lost and in need of help. This stranger eventually learns how to live in the new community since we behave towards him or her as equal to us. So Korczak wonders: why don't we do the same with children? We must treat children with respect, and listen to them, as peer. Maybe we don't remember it, but once we were children too.

> Respect for the minutes of the present. How will he know how to live tomorrow if we prevent him from living a responsible life today? Do not make the child a slave of tomorrow.[327]

It is in this sentence that I found a deep connection with Korczak, namely the sense of equality and the idea at the base of storytelling: "When I talk or play with a child, an instant of my life joins an instant of his and these two moments have the same dignity".[328]

We should abandon the idea to mould a perfect human being for the future, and as I mentioned so far in this dissertation, through other educators and philosopher, also according to Korczak we must live here and now. To do this, if we really want to give a better future to them, we need to work on ourselves, thinking about how we can relate to them, because as Korczak says if we want to build a solid house, we need to have a solid ground, and this ground is built today, not tomorrow when the roof will be built.

According to Korczak, the educator must be a person not simply specialized in pedagogical and psychological practices, but he should also have a broad culture to give the answers that the educatees seek. Educators must accompany the educatees on the path of growth, showing them the way, but educators must not impose their own thoughts, educators must instead help the educatees cultivate their own thought and individuality. To accomplish this, it is evident that the educator must conceive the others, the children, as equals, having a relationship of equality with them. Even in the book *How to love a Child*[329], Korczak speaks of the children and their coming into the world. The basic thesis of this dissertation focuses on the adult-child relationship which, according to Korczak, is unequal, and unbalanced to the advantage of the adult and to the disadvantage of the child, as I pointed out previously. He explains how the adult takes up all the space. This involves a capillary control over the child, seen as a table to be set, a blank sheet to be filled, and an irrational being to be taught. The child hardly listens to the adult and for this reason, children are considered rebels.[330]

Anyway, this rebellious attitude is seen positively by Korczak; precisely this characteristic is considered the most useful resource for their growth. A natural reinforcement in a society where the law of the fittest, of the strongest is enforced, and this just rebellion on the part of children, as perceived by Korczak, can be the medicine to face a society that is not always fair.

Nevertheless, it's important to approach Korczak's words with caution. He indeed advocates against fostering a child who grows into an adult wielding strength to oppress. Instead, he envisions a child who is sensitive, emotionally aware, adept at dialogue and critical thinking, capable of forming independent ideas and perspectives, and open to listening and accepting others. It was a difficult mission, if not impossible, especially in the period in which Korczak wrote and worked, a period where dialogue, kindness and help towards others were not so common, a world that had fallen into the abyss of atrocities. All this, however, must not make the educator lose the desire to help the child look at the world of adults, with all its problems. Even because children are capable and conscious, much more than adults may think.

It is necessary to place trust in the children's actions related to their aptitudes and encourage the growth of the mind and curiosity.[331] However, it is also important to underline that Korczak does not expect an adult world to be forcibly transformed into a world like that of children, but he wishes that adults become accomplices of children. The educator must deal with slow and conscientious work, a work that requires great effort on the part of all the interpreters involved, from the educator to the child. Only through listening, reflection, and acceptance of the other, can life experiences be faced, giving the children the opportunity to organize themselves. Arkel, in his reading of Korczak's work, suggests that in "the educational practice the children are the first ring of the chain".[332] Everything begins from them. Children help educators because they are interested to do things correctly, with care.

We must overcome mistrust, we must accept children as they are, without conditions. Korczak writes: "To know how we should do it, we have to turn to experts, and the experts, in this case, are ... the children".[333] In other words, one must put everything behind oneself and become a true travel companion of the children, be *with* them, but *not like* them. Korczak's work is used to underline the difficulty of the child in the relationship with the world, but also the difficulty that adults have with children, a difficulty often born from a series of prejudices and preconceptions. We as adults should w/o/a/nder with them.

It is true that every age has its own development but this development cannot be hierarchical, different degrees of maturity are wrongly attributed, as there are no gradations in the field of feelings, whatever they may be. Even nowadays, how many times do you hear adults say to children, "when you grow up you will understand this or that..." as if love, pain, joy, and the discoveries felt by children are less true, less strong because they are felt in a smaller body. Korczak asks adults to understand that the child's "time" is different from their own. Adult time does not overlap with the time of the child, which is a time that becomes a river that flows fast, a river that observes and is observed. Korczak suggests it with this metaphor:

> We paint it with exaggeratedly dark colors and then the day comes when our predictions become reality: the house collapses because we have neglected the foundations.[334]

The foundations are obviously the children. Here we grasp the paradox of education, we try to educate the child to become an adult, to enter the adult world as soon as possible, precisely that world, however, so much criticized and painted in dark colours by the adults themselves. So, is it not better to let the child grow free, in the hope that the man of tomorrow can change the dusky colours and create a world full of bright colours?[335] The adults must rethink their role, their relationship with the child.

Although Korczak was not an avowed anarchist, he can certainly be associated with anarchism through his educational example. His example was so important that the Convention on the Rights of the Child took inspiration from his writings. His radical humanism transcends time and space, and as an educator, I cannot but reflect on his educational work.

One last thought

In *Stories of the Night* by Kitty Crowther,[336] there is a story where a character throws stones into the lake, stones on which he draws or writes stories. I imagine these authors as the stones of the tale, stones with a story written on them, thrown into the water to form concentric circles which intersect with each other and form new stories and accommodate the concept of *equality* between these circles.

Once again stories have been the focus. As an autoethnographic work, stories are both the subject and the object of my investigation, nonetheless a precious tool to investigate. Through others' stories, which are not intended to be imitated but rather should arise in us questions and reflections, I proposed a sort of dialogue, as it is life itself. A dialogue between educators and between adults and children, through *educational praxis* that starts from *equality.*

This chapter aimed to underline that equality is not only a philosophical concept, but it is a way of life. What I mean is that each of these authors tried to live according to equality.

The authors used in this chapter and dissertation share the concept of *ontological equality.* My point is that despite these differences of space, time and circumstances, we have the possibility in our daily practice to suspend inequality and drive through equality. In other words, I believe it is naïve to assume that equality prevails throughout society, a reality evident in our daily experiences. However, despite this, we can cultivate such an environment within schools. The intention is not to shape a child solely for future adulthood, but rather to utilize this educational space as a mean of extending the opportunities it offers beyond the school setting.

Instead, when we think in a chronological way, we delegate the concept of equality to the future, while we should think in aionic way, which means here and now, as only the present is the home of equality. This is, I think, another approach to education, instead of thinking and practicing for the future, we should practice for the present. Storytelling, being a story in its very essence, can foster equality on several levels and can help us, as educators, remain in the present.

Notes

[274] Freire, Paulo. *Letters to Cristina.* (New York: Routledge, 1996).

[275] Rancière, Jacques. *Il Maestro Ignorante.* (Milano: Mimesis Edizioni, 2008).

[276] Kohan 2014, p.44.

[277] Kohan 2018.

[278] Interesting here to read Matthews 1980, 1984, 1994.

[279] Franco, Lorenzoni. *Educare Controvento.* (Palermo: Sellerio, 2023), p.13.

[280] Ibanez, Tomás. *Anarchia in Movimento.* (Milano: Eleuthèra Edizioni, 2014).

[281] Ibanez 2014, p.33.

[282] Ibanez 2014.

[283] Mortari 2008.

[284] Kohan 2014.

[285] Kohan 2018.

[286] Lorenzoni 2009.

[287] Rancière 2007.

[288] Ingold 2018.

[289] Rancière 2007; Kohan 2014.

[290] Rancière 2007.

[291] Freire 2014c.

[292] Here for example one can see Freire 200, 2018, 2019.

[293] Rancière 2008, p.39.

[294] Kohan 2021, p.43.

[295] Worth to notice that Colin Ward, 1991, argues against those biographies/autobiographies that are perfect, he says they are unreliable, since life is not perfect, and so we can't learn something new.

[296] Kohan 2014.

[297] Kohan 2014.

[298] Kohan 2014, p.91.

[299] Kohan 2014.

[300] Kohan 2014, p.111.

[301] Kohan 2014.

[302] Malaguzzi 2016.

[303] Kohan 2021, p.48.

[304] Kohan 2021.

[305] Kohan, Walter. *Infanzia e filosofia.* (Perugia: Morlacchi editore), 2006.

[306] Kohan 2006; Pacini-Ketchabaw and Taylor 2015b.

[307] Kohan 2006, p.11.

[308] Ingold 2018; Freire 2014c.

[309] Kohan 2006.

[310] Kohan 2006, 2014; Caputo, 2020.

[311] Kohan and Waksman 2013; Caputo 2020.

[312] Kohan, 2006, p.xvii.

[313] Kohan, 2006, p.15.

[314] Kohan, 2021.

[315] Kohan, 2006; Caputo 2020.

[316] Kohan, Walter. Paulo Freire and the Childhood of a Philosophical and Educational Life in *Thinking, Childhood and Time.* Walter Omar Kohan and Barbara Weber (ed.), 131–143, (London: Lexington Books), 2020.

[317] Kohan 2020, p.135.

[318] Kohan, Walter. *Childhood, Education and Philosophy.* (New York: Routledge), 2015, p.45.

[319] Sìmon Rodríguez changed for some time his name in Samuel Robinson. During his journey in Europe, he decided to change name to see the world with different eyes, once back in Latin America he took back his old name.

[320] In order to write this introduction to Korczak I have looked at the work of Dario Arkel, *Ascoltare la Luce* ,2009 and Janusz Korczak, *Il Diario dal Ghetto,* 1997.

[321] Korczak, Janusz. *The Child's Right to Respect.* (Washington: University Press of America, 1992).

[322] Korczak 2004, p.29.

[323] Korczak 2004, p.29.

[324] Korczak 2004.

[325] Korczak 1992.

[326] Korczak 2004, p.53.

[327] Korczak 2004, p.59.

[328] Korczak 2004, p.60.

[329] Korczak, Janusz. *How to Love a Child and Other Selected Works. Vol 1–2.* Elstree: Vallentine Publisher, 2018.

[330] Korczak 2004, 2013.

[331] Arkel, Dario. *Ascoltare la Luce.* (Ati editore, 2009).

[332] Arkel 2009, p.59.

[333] Korczak 2004, p.60.

[334] Korczak 2004, p.80.

[335] Korczak 2004.

[336] Crowther, Kitty. *Storie della Notte.* (Milano: Topipittori, 2008).

Teaching demands happiness and hope.
Paulo Freire.

Love is a combination of care, commitment, knowledge, responsibility,
respect and trust.
bell hooks

Being oppressed means the absence of choices.
bell hooks

Honesty and openness are always the foundation of insightful dialogue.
bell hooks

CHAPTER SEVEN

In quest with Paulo Freire

When I began to study pedagogy and philosophy at the university, I encountered many authors and many theories, yet most of them spoke neither to the heart nor to the mind. I read interesting theories, but none of them really engaged me. I could not find a way to make them my own, to put them into practice. I would study them for exams, but then they would end up in the drawer. One day, however, Freire knocked on my door. Since then, he has accompanied me everywhere, to university, in my experiences as an educator in Italy and Sweden, and I could even say in my daily life as a citizen and a father. In this thesis, he is the only author who has been with me since the very first day of my doctoral studies.

Although I have already mentioned Freire in this dissertation, I will give him special attention in this chapter. As mentioned, I have used Freire's work as a starting point for my educational practice in early childhood, even if his work has always been related within adult education. However, his principles can be reused in any educational context.

Paulo Freire was born in Brazil in 1921 from a middle-class family. He experienced poverty and hunger during the great depression of 1929. This event will mark him for the rest of his life, and it will be the basis from which his thoughts on poverty and his educational vision will spring. Freire begins studying at the university of his hometown, Recife, in the Faculty of Law, and simultaneously studies philosophy and psychology of language. He becomes a lawyer but he never practices the legal profession, instead he starts teaching Portuguese in secondary schools. In 1946 he became director of the Department of Education and Culture of the Social Service in the State of Pernambuco. Particularly engaged with the illiterate, he approaches the experience of liberation theology (at that time in Brazil, education was required in order to vote). In 1961 he was appointed director of the Department for Cultural Expansion of the University of Recife, and with this role he began to put his educational theories into practice. The Brazilian government, seeing the rapid results obtained by Freire, decides to finance his educational projects, opening thousands of cultural clubs throughout the State. The coup of 1964 puts an end to this educational effort, Freire is arrested as a traitor and imprisoned for two months, then he leaves the country to travel to Bolivia and then to Chile, where he lived and worked for five years. Freire's first book, *Education as a Free Practice*, was published in 1967, and it received excellent comments, so much so that he was invited as a visiting professor at Harvard University. *Pedagogia do Oprimido*, his most famous writing, was written in 1968, and was translated into Spanish and English in 1970 but published in Brazil only in 1974. In those years Freire was invited everywhere, he worked from Geneva to Cambridge, from Guinea Bissau to Africa. Freire returned to Brazil in 1979 and joined the Workers' Party in the city of Sao Paulo. Between 1980 and 1986, he played the role of supervisor on his own adult literacy project. With the victory in the municipal elections of the Workers' Party, Freire was appointed Secretary of Education for the State of Sao Paulo. The Paulo Freire Institute was founded in 1991 with the aim of developing and elaborating Freire's theories on popular education.

Freire can help us do three things. One, to understand and put into practice the concept of w/o/a/ndering. Two, to give some theoretical and practical tools to support anarchist education. Three, to deepen the concept of equality.

Another thing I would like to emphasize is that Freire never called himself an anarchist. However, several commentators like Colin Ward, Robert Haworth and Judith Suissa mentioned Freire in their works where also anarchism is mentioned.[337] Authors such as Chomsky have also devoted insights into Freire's work.[338] An anarchist reader, if put in front of Freire's work, would hardly reject it in its entirety. In the first part of the chapter, in developing Freire's thoughts, I decided to use the format of a dialogue, and I was inspired by his book *We Make the Road by Walking*, which is a long conversation with the social educator Myles Horton.[339]

In the fictive conversation that Freire and I will engage in, we will speak about some concepts that are at the foundation of his philosophy, but overall, we speak about Freire's understanding about the role of the educator. I continue what I started with Colin Ward. In the second part, taking inspiration from his letters to his niece Cristina, I wrote him three letters, where I will delve into his pedagogical philosophy.

In dialogue with Paulo Freire

I felt as if it was time to go to Città Alta, I needed some fresh air. I left the sheets regarding the introduction to this chapter on the table since I needed to clear out ideas. It's never easy to tackle authors that had a huge impact on you.

Anyway, I hoped that my hike up the hill of the old town in Bergamo could inspire me. It was chilly, the leaves from the trees began to change colours, the air smelt of embers, the chestnuts were in a pan on the fire, in short, autumn had arrived. The view of the Alps is always beautiful. I sighed.

Why are you sighing? Someone asked me.

Me: *I don't know, I'm getting some air and thinking about how beautiful the world is.*

The gentleman who had just sat next to me on the bench had a beard and wore glasses.

But where had I seen him before?

Me: *Excuse me, I'll say something crazy, but you look so familiar... you look like... Paulo Freire... could you...?*

Paulo: *Yes, I am. I was visiting Reggio Emilia to see how it has changed since my last visit in 1993. Always a fascinating educational reality, I must say. But how do you know who I am? I'm certainly not a Hollywood actor or a rock star...*

Me: *You won't believe me, but I'm actually writing a chapter about your work. Or rather, a reflection chapter on some of your concepts and intentions regarding education.*

Paulo: *So, let's hear what you want to write, and if you would like to, we can discuss it.*

Me: *I'm writing my doctoral thesis in pedagogy. Up to this point I have written about a w/o/a/ndering approach, I have written about Colin Ward's thinking, and displayed the philosophical pedagogy of some educators and their understanding of equality. I found your educational philosophy very close to practical reality. But it is also a philosophy that is, as Kohan defines it, a pedagogical philosophy of the question, rather than a pedagogical philosophy of the answer.*

Paulo: *Indeed, in my writings I try to describe a reality, my reality (which is also why I always repeat it is important to rethink my philosophy and not replicate it the same), but at the same time my reflections lead to questions, to reflections on our educational practice as educators.*[340]

Me: *Exactly, this is also what I am interested in with my work. I propose reflections more than solutions since these can vary depending on the circumstances.*

Paulo: *I see. And what about Colin Ward? Was he not an anarchist?*

Me: *Yes. I found his position about childhood, school and educators very interesting. I could relate many of his ideas to your own. In reading your work, I noticed that you often use the term* progressive educators, *I think I could include anarchist educators as well. Anyway, as Kohan, I don't like dogmatism, so when one tries to set a dogma, to radicalize the thinking, s/he loses credibility in my eyes.*

Paulo: *I agree with you. In* Pedagogia do Autonomia *I clearly state that I have bias, that I take a stand about some argument, and take a clear position and I stated this also to the students. However, I let the others speak, because even through dialogue we can make an educational practice.*

Me: *There are so many concepts I would like to speak to you about, but mainly educators.*

Paulo: *Where would you like to begin?*

Me: *Maybe we could begin speaking about equality. It's a concept that I find interesting.*

Paulo: *Sure. Why? What caught your attention about equality?*

Me: *I suppose it's because I speak about equality in my thesis through the work of other authors, and also because it is a pillar in anarchist pedagogical philosophy.*

Paulo: *Let me say that nobody is superior to anyone else, and it is one the few certainties that I am sure of, further we have to accept and respect what is different.*[341]

Me: *I totally agree with you. It has been this vision, this understanding, that brought me closer to anarchism.*

Paulo: *It is important that educators start putting equality into practice by listening to students.*[342]

Me: *This is not an easy task. In this moment I speak as an educator in early childhood education and as a father. From one side there are expectation from society, the policy makers, to produce something tangible, concrete, that one* *can touch. This situation compresses the space for listening. In my years as an educator, I have often found myself unable to listen to children as I wished, because we needed to deliver, to show to parents or headmaster what we did during the week, a continuous flow of information to give around, a continuous documentation to be produced. It's a bit different at home, I don't need to document or produce something to show, still society expects a certain number of activities that have to be done with your children, more than in school. Also, as a student, I have seldomly felt heard, doesn't matter where I was.*

Paulo: *I understand you. It is not easy to find this time. But I would like to stress my idea that we are ontologically equal.[343] So, it is something* a-priori.

Me: *This lets me think about a juxtaposition that is often made between you and Rancière. Something that I don't understand. Some readers like Biesta, Lewis and Bingham suggest, juxtaposing your idea of equality to Rancière idea of equality.[344] Where your is an equality a-posteriori, while Rancière's idea is a-priori. I believe and agree with Kohan that your notion of equality is a-priori too.[345] Then Kohan suggests, "if teachers and students are equal from the get-go, what then is the purpose of education?"[346]*

Paulo: *And how do you solve this problem?*

Me: *I acknowledge that it's a complex issue. Regarding equality in education, as Kohan emphasizes, it's inherently political. We need to consider the ontological dimension of equality, which asserts that every individual is inherently equal. However, politically, we selectively acknowledge certain prerequisites for equality. In essence, it is politics that determines the criteria for considering others as equals. That's why I perceive both you and Rancière as having a sensitivity overlapping with the concept of equality in anarchism. Anarchists hold that all individuals are equal, serving as the foundational principle from which we can embark on an educational, political, or any other form of relationship.*

Paulo: *Ok, but as an educator when you are in a class, how do you put this equality into practice? As an educator, you have a power that comes from your position as a teacher, for instance.*

Me: *Sometimes I feel that it is not simple to follow anarchist's suggestions. For this reason, maybe, I look with interest to Ward's work and to the concept of daily anarchism or pockets of anarchism. But as a teacher I must remember that the child in front of me, and I think of Korczak here, is not less than me just because s/he is smaller.[347]*

Paulo: These are understandable claims, and I agree with you. But in practice, how do you approach such an education?

Me: In early childhood settings we are lucky, despite some issues we also a flexibility in planning our spaces, time and activities so if as educators want to foster this concept of equality, we can always find space and time to do it. For example, there are times in preschool where children play freely, in that moment as an educator I could keep a distance from play, I could decide not to be involved, to say to children what do or not to do, or I could sit on the floor with them and participate in their play.

Paulo: But then is it not you as an educator the one who controls the play? And then, what about your anarchist approach?

Me: Of course, as I said, anarchist educators are involved in the process of education. Let me explain. We must not get confused with a laissez faire approach, where we leave children on their own to self-educate. When I play with children, I play by their rules and I also participate in their decision-making. I take my cue from what Marc Armitage says about playworkers.

Paulo: Exactly, I also stress this out too. An educator always takes a stand, s/he is not neutral. Education is a political act.[348] *But what about Armitage?*

Me: Paulo, you need to know that I approached education many years ago as a playworker, then after several circumstances I became a preschool teacher and pedagogista. But my first experience taught me so much, and I practiced, and practice, with a playworker attitude. Anyway, Armitage says that it's not our job to lead or dictate children's play. We can't say what or how children should play. Then Armitage affirms that "the role of a playworker is seen as one who produced for the right condition".[349]

Paulo: I have a question, what about the right condition?

Me: He means that playworkers, and I could say preschool teachers or educators, should provide the right space for the play of children. It's not something new, Malaguzzi states that environment is the third educator, and the Reggio Emilia approach gives great importance to the environment where children spend most of their daytime, the school.

Paulo: Absolutely, I believe it is the structure, the matrix where we are, that replicates inequalities. But what about play and anarchism, I suspect that Armitage is an anarchist or anyway he sympathizes with anarchism.

Me: Yes, Armitage underlines how during his education in the 80s, many play-workers had sympathies or close ideas to anarchism. He interestingly suggests analogies between play and anarchy highlighting the essence of anarchism: decentralizing decision-making, addressing power dynamics, and constantly questioning established norms. By equating the free-spirited nature of a playing child with the principle of anarchy, we emphasize the role of play in urban settings as a form of anarchy in action.[350]

Paulo: I see, very interesting.

Me: To recap. When I play with children I'm doing a political act, I decide to share with them a common experience, I decide that we are equal. The way I think about the environment is another political act.

Paulo: In which way?

Me: As educators we can decide together with children or for the children how a classroom should look like. If children need to ask permission to do something, for example if every time they want to paint, they need to ask permission to some adults, then they will have restrictions. If they can paint when they want it's possible to build another kind of relationship. Of course, there are exceptions, e.g. in a classroom where there are children of different ages ranging from 1 year to 5, some toys not suitable for younger children must be placed in positions where there is control over who can use them. Otherwise, it is only fair that children can experiment. And in play I see not only an anarchist practice, or an act of storytelling, but I see your idea of equality, praxis, dialogue, and so much more. But play, as every human practice based on relationship, can hide the problem of power, where some child takes over other children. For this reason, it is important to show to children how to create a relationship grounded in respect, empathy and listening.

Paulo: I understand. Unfortunately, I must go now, I have a train to catch. However, I really liked our conversation, so can I ask you a favour?

Me: Absolutely, what can I do for you?

Paulo: I'm an old man, so I would really appreciate it if you could send me a letter with some of your reflections about my work and your work.

Me: This is a great idea. I will write some lines this evening. Have a nice trip back home. Or maybe it will be me who will do a journey back to the future.

In the second chapter of this thesis, I wrote that I am on a quest to find my voice not only in terms of content but also in the way I write. In the chapter on anarchism and in this one I tried to write two dialogues to expound and develop some ideas of Colin Ward and Paulo Freire. In other chapters I wrote personal experiences, more autoethnographic in nature. Instead, in the second part of this chapter I attempted to address some of Freire's educational-philosophical themes through the writing of letters addressed to him. Letters have always fascinated me, I think for example of the letters my grandfather wrote to his family from the front during WWII, and despite the difficulties they somehow managed to communicate. I grew up in a time where there was no Internet, mobile phones, and the frenzy of communication of today. I still remember when, to invite someone to play, you either phoned them at home, hoping they were there, or you went straight to their house and knocked on the door. As a child I remember a project I did with the school, I had a pen pal from another school, in our case in Romania, and every month I would write, like my classmates, to our pen pals, and we would wait for their reply. In general, however, I always wrote a lot of letters. Then this composition has been surely influenced by Freire's book *Letters to Cristina,* where he wrote several letters to his niece about his life, his w/o/a/n-dering. So, I thought I would write three letters to Freire. These letters were written knowing that I did not expect a reply, but with the intention of being able to reorganise my thoughts on certain questions. Letters that will perhaps receive a reply in the near future. In any case, the stylistic form of the letter allows a certain flexibility of exposition, and this allowed me to take a step forward in the search for my own voice.

In the first letter, through an autoethnographic example, I discuss the importance of listening, the possibilities that storytelling give us to create a philosophical research community and the importance of taking the time to philosophise. In the second letter, I discuss the importance of everyone's diversity, the importance of being attentive to the other, and thinking about education not based on banking education, but on problem-posing practice. Only in this way can we avoid a transformation of the school that now tends towards standardisation. In the third letter, I take up the idea of storytelling and how it is intertwined with the practice of problem-posing. Through storytelling we can dialogue with the other, we can relate to the world and instead of being in the world, we are with the world.

First Letter

Dear Paulo,

I hope this letter finds you well. As you asked me to do, here I am writing this first letter about my reflections on education. As an educator I have always given attention to storytelling since stories, play and philosophizing meet in it, and I always practice or foster the practice with the idea to do with *rather than* for.

One day at work I had with me a book by Shaun Tan[351], The lost thing. As every Tan's work, this picture book is beautifully drawn, and the story has as a deep meaning. Tan's story portrays a boy who is out and about in a city, a big city, a modern, grey, leaden, I would say dystopian city, like the ones you see in science fiction films, or some modern suburbs. In his roaming the boy finds an object, a living object. But he doesn't know what to do with it, he doesn't know where to put it, who is it? The boy sees that it is different, but he does not know how to help it become what it is supposed to be.

Through a series of vicissitudes, he eventually manages to find a place just outside the city, where the lost thing finally finds itself, and finally it can express itself for what it is. Of the many interpretations that can be given to this story, I prefer this one: it is about working to make every human being go to a world where everyone can become fully himself and is welcomed as such, even if it is a difficult world to reach. From the leaden, grey, conformist atmosphere where everything is the same and nothing has a life of its own, it is a matter of finding the right path, but to do this you need someone to act as a go-between: praise the educator. In short, on the one hand I conceive an anarchic educator, who is there to help each child to find his or her individuality, and on the other hand a criticism of the conformist society.

Anyway, I didn't plan to read this story, it was a couple of children who, intrigued by Tan's book, asked to leaf through it. Once they had turned the first, second and third page, the number of children had increased... before long we were all sitting on the floor reading Tan's story aloud. It was afternoon and soon parents would come to pick up children, so we put the book away, but I promised to keep it at school. The next day we read the story again and so we did for the whole week. Consistency is a perfect tool to nurture curiosity. As I remember, in Pedagogia da Autonomia *you suggest that every human being is immersed in a matrix of curiosity. The role of the educator is to remove the obstacles that the educatees might encounter in the w/o/a/ndering through their curiosity.*

At that time there was a very good educational possibility, the possibility to open a more philosophical discussion, to open the possibility of developing the story. I was already thinking of questions, of things to do. I then stopped. I was reasoning like an educator who wanted to bring home a "result" to show, an educator who had a clear plan for the children to carry out. I took a deep breath and decided to postpone every single decision until the following week. However, this story brought me to think about the possibility to "reading the word and the world"[352]. *I was interested in seeing the w/o/a/ndering that could arise from it.*

Over the next few weeks, we started to create a project, all together. As an educator I was with them in this project, I was not an observing educator, detached, I was a participating educator. However, I noticed once again how it is difficult to be attentive and how it is difficult to empty us... to move around.[353] *The children were interested in the story of this lonely object and our story-telling moved forward. In our w/o/a/ndering, we philosophised about many aspects. Retrospectively, I had some anarchist hints without even realizing it.*

In my notes, I annotated these reflections of mine intertwined with some in-put and dialogues with the children.[354] *When reading* The Lost Thing[355] *I thought that the boy and the lost thing challenged the rules of their world, which I can understand as an act of anarchism. These reflections arose not from a "proper" philosophical dialogue but from our creative moments with clay*[356] *and through play.*

Me: *what do you think about this story?*

Roberto: *The lost thing looks so weird, but the boy helps it anyway.*

Monica: *it's like he doesn't care about what others think.*

I agree and I could see how the boy challenged the societal norms of his world by caring for something that others consider strange or out of place, this act of kindness is like an act of rebellion against the norms.

Monica interrupted my thoughts: the lost thing doesn't belong anywhere in the world of the story...

Me: *and how do you feel about this?*

Monica: *I feel sad...*

Roberto: *when I lose something I am sad...*

Luigi: *maybe also the lost thing is sad... being lost...*

Monica: *luckily there is the boy that found it...*

Roberto: *so, it is no longer alone...*

I think to the boy and the thing that find a place, and it's like they're creating their own little world, is it not what we should strive as educators and children, to create our world, to rethink society outside and to imagine something different?

Roberto later in the discussion, when moulding some clay to build a house to the boy, exclaimed: they create a world just the way they want it! With their own rules.

This brought me to think that the boy and the lost thing can be themselves without conforming to the world's standard... but in this reflection I also felt a bit of discomfort. Does it make sense to relate this story to anarchism? I think it does, I mean that anarchism wants to avoid conforming to the world's standards, imposed from elsewhere, but it demands a common place, a common ground to build up a community to share a common horizon. A horizon where near the I, stays the WE. Where there is the possibility for individuality to arise. And this is what the lost thing is looking for, it's individuality.

In my notes there is this quote from Monica: the boy and the lost thing, they don't talk with words...

Me: *like two people from different countries that don't know each other languages and speak through gesture...*

Luigi: *or like small children that don't speak yet...*

This discussion about language is interesting, how can we communicate with others? How can we create a dialogue? How can we tell stories? Sometimes, as a father and as an educator, I find myself a bit deaf to children voices. I recognize that I'm not attentive as Ingold encouraged us to be.[357] *To be attentive is a skill like every human act, like painting, like running, like cooking, and it needs to be trained. I remember when I began my journey into philosophy with children, I always had a note with questions to ask. The dialogue wasn't a real dialogue. It was more of a sort of interrogation. I chose an argument, I introduced it, I asked questions one after another. I was happy at the very beginning, I felt like I did "my" work. I had a notebook full of questions and answers. Then*

I realized that all of that didn't make any sense. I was stressed out, because I had to perform, I had to produce. The children weren't happy either, they thought it was pretty boring. Without considering that not every child develops language in the same way, in the same moment, some of them were excluded. So, I began to think to your perspective, Paulo, dialogue isn't just about words; it's about understanding and learning from each other... the boy and the lost thing have non-verbal connection, and they learn from each other through their actions and empathy. My philosophical practice switched in a more unstructured approach, every moment was a good moment to invite children to a critical thinking, through play, art, storytelling. Everyone could speak his or her language and could be listened from others.

I noted this comment from Roberto: the boy also listens to the lost thing, even when others don't...

Monica: *I would like that...*

Me: *that...?*

Monica: *that we could listen more...*

Me: *do you believe that the boy shows respect for the lost thing's thoughts and feelings?*

Monica: *I do...*

I think that even a short conversation can open reflections on our side as educators, it seemed to me that children asked to be heard, that they didn't feel to be heard. How many times have I thought that I could understand and feel them?

The boy in the story doesn't impose his will but listens and understands the thing. In the story then, it is shown that learning can happen through interactions with others, not just in a formal setting. Education is a lifelong journey. The boy and the lost thing don't just accept the world as it is; they try to make it better. Don't you agree, Paulo?

The conversations I had with children arose spontaneously, and in my Philosophy with Children practice, I always try wherever possible to encourage a spontaneous philosophizing moment. Even if this process, as I said, was not so smooth at the beginning of my practice. Also, because I always find it a bit complicated to claim that children are natural philosophers and, in this, I agree with Kohan.[358] *In our project not all the children expressed themselves verbally about the story, but they expressed themselves in other ways, for example through play, by asking others questions... and from there another conversation could begin. Through this experience, albeit retrospectively, I tried to think about you Paulo and about Colin Ward's close approach of everyday anarchism. I tried to be there with them, to create the conditions and at the same time to learn from them.*[359] *I underline how stories, play and philosophy acted as one. The words of Lorenzoni come to mind here, it's important to stay around stories a long time in order to have the* "*opportunity to investigate, deepen and unravel a great number of themes, tackling them from multiple points of view*".[360] *In other words, to stay in an aionic time.*[361] *Anyway, I must go now. Hope this letter of mine wasn't too long. It has been an important way to rethink my practice.*[362]

Warmly,
Matteo

Second letter

Dear Paulo,

Thank you for your answer to my first letter. I hope you are doing well. I'm writing to you because I've been thinking and I am more and more concerned about how the school tends to exclude; school is becoming a place where there is an attempt to quantify the intelligence in order to select individuals. But intelligence cannot be quantified.[363] *Rancière said that it is impossible to affirm that all intelligence are equal*[364] *and I think this is an important argument. It can be argued how the techno-political apparat tries to rank the manifestation of intelligence according to the scule that has been promoted in our society. We can think to all the tests that children and students are subjected nowadays, like the Pisa test. This way progressive politics try to present equality as a goal – generally a never-fully achievable goal – for the future rather than as a premise on which to build an egalitarian society.*[365]

Here then I can also think about a criticism to the standardization in the school. In Pedagogia da Autonomia, *you suggest that educators who have a democratic vision of their practice cannot escape the duty to insist on critical thinking, and overall, on the curiosity and autonomy of the educatee. It is possible to see this when you encourage, despite the limitation of the school, the ones who* make *the school daily: the educators, and when you welcome the students respecting their experiences, not only the experiences acquired at school but outside the school too.*[366] *I feel, and I agree with Masschelein and Simons, that public school is under attack and that we should defend it.*[367] *Masschelein and Simons say that in a good pedagogical relationship the inequalities that reign outside are suspended or interrupted. So as Kohan suggests it's our responsibility as educators to foster the practice of equality.*[368] *Maybe it is better to talk about the understanding of equality, showing it in our practice. This is also what an anarchist educator strives for. This is also how I read* The Lost Thing, *as a possible criticism to the school system.*

I understand this through your work Paulo, how you express in different ways the complexity of education, a practice that involves more than the relationship between educators and educatees, but the whole community as well. I appreciate how much you encourage us as educators to understand and to be curious about the educatees, their culture and their background. At the same time, it is important to show to the educatees who we are as educators, to show that we have our circumstances too.

You criticised the way governments decide the contents that must be taught at school. If it is only the government which decides what one must learn, the local community is nullified and oppressed, there is no possibility to use our own will or curiosity to grow. I understand your position as being very close to anarchism, where the State is questioned and what it is asked is a decentralization that will make it possible to listen carefully to each community.

As an educator in preschool sometimes I felt the difficulty to follow the curriculum, because not always, I would say seldomly, the reality and the demands from the curriculum are compatible. As educators, for example, we are obliged to have a certain type of pedagogical documentation, a well-documented type of work to show to the parents and the administrators, but these demands do not consider the children's time, their interests. It is important so to discuss with them, and relate their lives to their circumstances, as you suggest it is a fundamental aspect of rational thinking and it involves being open to risk and embracing novelty without dismissing it solely because it's unfamiliar, just as one shouldn't discard the old solely because it's no longer new chronologically.[369]

For example, in the previous letter, I talked to you about the project that was carried out from the book The Lost Thing. *Do you remember it? What I haven't told you is that at the same time we needed to fulfil a certain number of worksheets and activities to be documented. To show a certain kind of teaching, of "proper content". Speaking with colleagues back then and with teachers now, I feel preschools are becoming more and more like schools, with parameters to follow, with just a few spaces for a slower time, where children can be listened seriously. In the practice of storytelling, I therefore see a possibility where educators and children discover a common world together, where curiosity builds the possibility of learning (knowing) for children and teachers. At their own pace.*

I am intrigued at how you argue that if we analyze the relationship between students and educators it is possible to see a narrative character, *where the educator is the narrator, and the student is a listening object. This narration you talk about is an educational act.*[370] *I often think to this narrative character, depicted in a negative way by you due to this false relationship. I always try to keep it in mind when I approach an educational practice, so as to avoid it. When I read the story of* The Lost Thing[371], *I tried to be open to dialogue, I tried to listen and to engage in a discussion with children. I do the same also when we play, when we wander around the city or the woods, even when we craft something. I suppose you used to do the same too.*

You have suggested a concept called banking education *that is the act where the teacher as an active subject* explains *and* fills *an* empty object, *the student. Interesting to see how you, Paulo, understand education as a narrative process but at the same time you are critical of the way this narration is conducted, told, and practiced.*

I know that you hope for the creation of a new kind of relationship between the educator and the educatee. A good educator should stimulate the creativity of the educatees, for this reason, we must avoid the methodology of banking education which minimize this human characteristic.[372]

To overcome the act of banking education you proposed the problem-posing *practice. The* problem-posing *approach is based on the concept of generative theme through which educators have the possibility to change the vertical patterns embedded in banking education.*[373] *A generative theme opens the possibility to establish a real dialogue between educators and students, the latter will no longer be just spectators, and the former will not be just protagonists, students are now critical co-investigators in dialogue with the teachers.*[374] *Through this practice it is possible to create and re-create the world. In this way educatees, as well as educators, can view the world not as a fixed reality, but as a dynamic entity in constant process and transformation.*[375] *It is possible to appreciate this approach through a practice grounded in storytelling and w/o/a/ndering, a practice that looks at anarchism.*

For the educator, to use a generative theme, it is necessary that the educatees listen carefully, in this way the educator can propose an object of investigation and both educatees and educators can relate to this object. A generative theme fosters reflections, dialogues, criticism, and a culture which becomes a useful tool for social emancipation. Thanks to problem-posing practice and the use of generative themes, teachers and students become subjects of the educational process. The world, no longer merely a subject of deceptive description, becomes the canvas upon which human beings enact transformative actions, leading to their own humanization.[376] This world encompasses not only the physical realm beneath our feet but also the narrative landscapes we create through storytelling. Oh, my children are calling me now! It must be bedtime; a storytelling moment is awaiting. I'll write you again soon.

Warmly,
Matteo

Third letter

Dear Paulo,

I'm getting used to writing these letters. In this third letter I would like to expose some ideas I have regarding storytelling and your work. For instance, you say that the word *is the foundation of the relationship between human beings.[377] I then add that narration is a human practice, to narrate you need dialogue, and dialogue is created with words, or anyway through some kind of verbal/non-verbal interaction.*

Storytelling can be understood through your praxis. When children, and educators, tell a story, perhaps through playing, they can act this telling moment through your praxis. The action of the story starts, then an encounter and a reflection on what happens, and finally the narrative action starts again. I go back here to the example of The Lost Thing *project, from this story we created other stories, we reflected on our circumstances, but not only children had to listen to me, I had to listen to them too, otherwise the risk of a monologue was high. The children that didn't speak, that didn't engage actively in verbal discussion, needed to be heard in another way, so my listening should have been more attentive, in order to give everyone, the same possibility to express themselves. I remember that a child didn't get involved in the conversation, he was always behind me, listening, but quiet, yet he needed to express himself. We found the way. We created a* Thing, *a thing different from that of Tan's book, but it was the conduit for his voice to be heard. Anyway, I see the importance of dialogue in your work when you argue that dialogue is an existential need. It is an act of creation.*[378]

In my dissertation, I have illustrated Walter Kohan's idea of schooling and philosophy, that is an act of creativity. The creative act allows me to find solutions to contingent situations, allows me to listen (at least in my intentions) to children and find with them, and not for them, a common educational path, a path that can be found through play, storytelling, and philosophising. Shaun Tan's book ignited this creative act, from this interest, we explored our contingent situation. I can't pretend, and probably didn't mean to do so, that each story we tell and listen in the class must be important, *sometimes stories are just nice moment of rest and relaxation. However, it is important to be attentive, because we never know when a story could create an act of w/o/a/ndering, a creative act, a* place of imagination.

In my practice I try to avoid an education based on the premises that could foster what you call dimension of the culture of silence.[379] *An education that is not made on horizontal but rather vertical relationships. From top to bottom, from the educator who narrates to the children who listen, in silence. Acting in this way, the educator removes the possibility for the children to w/o/a/nder. The experience is narrated or transmitted by the educator and is not done by the children together with the educator, in a dialogic and horizontal relationship. I understand this position also through the lenses of anarchism. A horizontal relationship is what anarchism seeks to propose as the constitutive practice of education. To propose such a practice, an equal conception between educators and children is clearly required.*

I agree with your idea of human beings who are not filled with the world but who fill the world, an education that is defined as problem-posing because it asks the human being to get involved with the world, and with others.[380] *An education that requires intentionality, an act of knowledge, this way a problematizing education is implemented. But who educates whom in a similar context? I know that you would reply that we are educated in a shared way, through the mediation of the world which becomes a dialogic object. Human beings cannot be understood as strangers to the world, but they are intrinsically intertwined with it. Human beings know they are incomplete, and the roots of education lie there.*[381]

To enhance this education, it is worth to think again to the problem-posing education. Such practice could be seen in the daily storytelling moment that children have, in a sense it is storytelling itself that carries a problematizing approach as ontology and epistemology, in a way maybe self-revealing and self-developing. Gottschall argues that: the land of make-believe resembles less of paradise and more of a struggle. Children's play isn't a means of avoidance; it directly engages with the challenges of human existence.[382]

As we can notice, in every story we can tell there is a problem, a theme to solve and this way we could understand, or it is better to say, rethink the problematizing education proposed by you and anarchism. One further consideration, the problem-posing education, as I understand and rethink, is not directly based on a narrative/narration act, it could be, but it sprouts from daily problems that educators and children face. This problem-posing education could be formulated through the practice of narration, which could also be seen as a practice of philosophising. You suggest, as Mortari and Ingold[383] do too, that humans are being in the making.[384] Anyway this form is a creative form, a continuous creating like the dialogue that is also an act of creation. It cannot be an act of conquest, of submission to the other, if anything a conquest of the world together with the other.

I understand how much you push us as educators to look for courage and solidarity, that is, to go beyond the fear of encounter with the other, through communion with the other, to which we do together with others. It is therefore possible to affirm, Paulo, that in your reflection education is also based through the practices of co-construction of knowledge. You stress the importance of differentiating the concept of being in the world, which is the condition of every living being, with being with the world, which is a specific human condition. When we are with the world, we can establish with others, with the reality in which we live, processes of communication and mutual influence. To be with the world it is necessary to develop a "transitive" consciousness that allows the communicative passage between the subject and the reality of the world in which he or she lives. From this openness to the world questions arise. It is from these premises that those models of educational, formative, and social intervention are born, based precisely on the active role of the subject. Anyway, I enjoyed writing these letters to you, and I appreciated your previous feedback. I hope I'll have the chance to do it again sometime in the future.

Yours,
Matteo

Summarizing Freire

In these pages I have introduced some of Freire's thoughts. In the way I arranged this chapter, my intention was to relate Freire to anarchism and w/o/a/ndering, as well as my practice as an educator in early childhood education. I proposed a reading of Freire through anarchism. Furthermore, I have tried, within my limits, to follow the path Freire traced, namely that of pedagogical and philosophical reflection on the work of the educator. Of his relationship with the world, of his relationship with the educated. In this specific case then, I tried, at Freire's invitation, to rethink his approach from the world of adults, the illiterate, and the oppressed, to the world of early childhood. In fact, I believe that the strength of Freire's thought lies in its plasticity, which really gives us the possibility to reinvent Freire's philosophy. His observations on the educational world, on the educational mode, touch every single educator, regardless of the context in which they work. When Freire urges us to be curious or ethical, no matter if we work with children or adults, in which school, or in which context, we have the possibility to try to be curious or ethical.

For example, when I worked with Shaun Tan's text, I created my own framework on some Freirean pillars such as problem-posing, dialogue, curiosity, listening; and in doing so I retraced Freire educational philosophical point of view. A knowledge built through a w/o/a/ndering. A w/o/a/ndering that does not hide the difficulties of being an educator. Perhaps it was precisely this intellectual honesty of Freire that brought me closer to his understanding of education. I think that, precisely through personal w/o/a/ndering, precisely in putting yourself out there day after day, the beauty of educational practice emerges. If we consider educational practice as doing the same thing every single day, then curiosity, joy and hope are lost. If, on the other hand, we consider educational practice as a doing and redoing, where each day is different from the one that precedes it and the one that follows it, curiosity and happiness are continually generated and regenerated. Certainly, as Freire encourages us to do, educating demands commitment and humility.

Notes

[337] Suissa 2010; Haworth 2014; Ward 2014.

[338] Conference on Paulo Freire and the pedagogy of the Oppressed at Harvard University: https://www.youtube.com/watch?v=2Ll6M0cXV54&t=1229s

[339] Horton, Myles and Freire, Paulo. *We Make the Road by Waling.* (Philadelphia: Temple University Press, 1990).

[340] Freire 2014.

[341] Freire 2000.

[342] Kohan, Walter. *Paulo Freire: a Philosophical Biography.* (London: Bloomsbury, 2021), p.23.

[343] Brandao, Carlos Rodriguez. Paulo Freire-a edução, a cultura e a universidade: memòria de uma história de cinquenta anos atrás. Revista festim, natal (1) 2, 2015. p. 157–172

[344] Biesta and Bingham 2010; Lewis 2012.

[345] Kohan 2021.

[346] Kohan 2021, p.21.

[347] Korczak 2004.

[348] Kohan, Walter. *Childhood, Education and Philosophy.* (New York: Routledge, 2015)

[349] Armitage, Marc. Playwork: the Anarchy Wing of Sociology. In *Education, Childhood and Anarchism. Talking Colin Ward.* Catherine Burke and Ken Jones (ed.), 113–123. (Ney York: Routledge, 2014), p.118.

[350] Armitage 2014, p.118

[351] Tan, Shaun. *The Lost Thing.* (London: Hodder Children's Books, 2010).

[352] Freire, Paulo and Macedo, Donaldo P. *Literacy: Reading the Word [and] the World.* (Routledge & Kegan Paul: London, 1987).

[353] Mortari 2006.

[354] The names of the children are fictive, in order to keep their anonymity.

[355] Tan 2010.

[356] Yes, also in this occasion I endorsed a w/o/a/ndering with clay.

[357] Ingold, Tim. *Anthropology and/as Education.* (New York: Routledge, 2018).

[358] Kohan, Walter. *Infanzia e Filosofia.* (Perugia: Morlacchi editore, 2006).

[359] Armitage, 2014.

[360] Lorenzoni 2023, p.117.

[361] Kohan 2020.

[362] See Masschelein 2010.

[363] See the previous chapter through Kohan and Rancière's understanding.

[364] Rancière 2008.

[365] Bingham and Biesta, 2010.

[366] I refere here to Kohan's *hacer escuela,* that we have encountered in *El Maestro Inventor, 2018.*

[367] Masschelein, Jan and Simons, Maarten. *In Defense of School.* (Leuven: Education, Culture and Society publishers, 2013)

[368] Kohan 2021.

[369] Freire 2014c.

[370] Freire 2013.

[371] Tan 2010.

[372] Freire 2014c.

[373] Freire, 2013.

[374] Freire, 2013.

[375] Freire, 2013.

[376] Freire, 2013.

[377] Freire and Macedo 1987.

[378] Freire 2013.

[379] Freire 2014c.
[380] Freire, 2013.
[381] Freire, 2013.
[382] Gottschall, Jonathan. *The Storytelling Animal: how Stories Make us Human.* (New York: Mariner Books, 2013).
[383] Mortari 2006; Ingold 2018.
[384] Freire 1990, 2013.

To have a place, to live and belong in a place, to live from a place without destroying it, we must imagine it. By imagination we see it illuminated by its own unique character and by our love for it. By imagination we recognize with sympathy the fellow members, human and nonhuman, with whom we share our place.
Wendell Berry

Imagination is what Providence uses to take men captive in actuality, in existence, in order to get them far enough out, or within, or down into existence. And when imagination has helped them get as far out as they should be – then actuality genuinely begins.
Søren Kierkegaard

CHAPTER EIGHT

Epilogue: in quest of *places of imagination*

A city, a camera and some grandparents

Every now and then I like to pamper myself, one of the ways I pampered myself at that time was to leave home early in the morning and go to the café near the school where I worked to have breakfast. I liked to sit at the table, read the newspaper and, in between sips of a cappuccino and bites of a brioche, I would greet the other regulars. That morning I was sitting, waiting for breakfast, when a voice from the other side of the café shouted: "Grandpa! Look, it's Matteo! My teacher! Let's go!" Grandpa didn't have time to fully understand the situation and found himself thrown at my table.

Grandpa: *Sorry about my grandson! I'll leave you to your breakfast!*

Me: *No! If you want to sit down, we can have breakfast together, no bother.*

Child: *Matteo, do you know that grandpa is really old? When he was my age the school where I go didn't exist!*

Me: *I can imagine.*

Grandpa: *Eh, actually when I was little, it was all rural here. Now the city has taken over. The landscape is certainly different.*

Me: *I wonder how different your life was!*

Grandpa: *I must be honest, in some ways it was better, but it was a difficult life, especially for our parents. It was the period right after World War II.*

Me: *What was school like?*

Grandpa: *I didn't go to preschool, I was home with my parents, I helped them to work, they were farmers. I and my nine siblings. Anyway, I think that schools are much better today. When my grandson comes home and tells me what you did at school, I'm so glad. This is something I didn't have in my childhood.*

Me: So, you didn't go to school at all?

Grandpa: I went to school when I was six, but after school I was busy to help my parents.

Me: I think that sometimes there is a bit of nostalgia for the old days, even when I talk to my grandparents or my parents, it always seems that their time was better. Even if it was a tough time.

Grandpa: I think it's really nostalgia of not being young anymore. Sure, there were some freedoms that children don't have today, like running in the meadows, now it's all car parks. Going to call other children in the village to play. Today it's the parents who must plan, among a thousand different activities. There is no spontaneity in the encounters. For sure there was another understanding of community. Now it is more an individualistic society.

Child: Grandpa, can we show Matteo the pictures you have of the village from when you were young?

Grandpa: I don't think he would be interested.

Me: Me? Of course I would! My grandparents were also into photography and so am I. I always go around with my camera and try to document life around me.

Grandpa: Then one day I'll bring you the photos.

Me: If you are not busy this afternoon, when you come to school to pick up your grandson you can bring the photo album and maybe we can see it together with all the other children.

Child: Yesssss!

Grandpa: Alright, let's do that.

The afternoon arrived, and so did Grandpa. In his hands he held a cardboard box, inside there were hundreds of photos. The children were intrigued by Grandpa and the box. We spent an hour looking at the pictures and guessing where they had been taken. How many stories in those pictures, how many questions, how many lives. Grandpa was kind enough to leave us several photos to keep.

The next day the children were still interested in the photos, and we decided to look at them. They had a lot of questions about how people lived back then, they imagined their grandparents' games, laughed at the funny cars or clothes they wore. I then asked if they wanted to hear more stories about those times. Of course they did. Then I thought about how to do it. I decided together with other colleagues to have a picnic with the grandparents so that they could tell us their stories.

The day of the picnic arrived. It went well. But the children wanted to know and understand even more about their grandparents' world. They had also heard stories where the adults, the teachers, punished the children. Stories where children worked in some farms or in factories and did not go to school. In short, they were not just images of happy children running through the fields, free. There were also images of sad children. A bit like the city that was getting bigger and bigger. A sad city, where there are few spaces for children, and sometimes even for grandparents.

What prompted my reflection was the children's perception of a magical, yet uncertain world depicted in the pictures. They seemed hesitant about fully embracing it. Moreover, they were acutely aware of the challenges in their own reality. While they acknowledged that children in their community attended school rather than working, they also recognized the constraints on their freedom. Or maybe it was a different kind of freedom.

One child said: I don't know who is freer, us or our grandparents?

Me: *In what sense? I asked... it was a bit of a difficult concept.*

Child: *Our grandparents could run around the countryside, but they could also be punished, they didn't always have new clothes or toys, and sometimes they only ate bread and milk.*

Me: *True.*

Child: *Whereas today we can eat, dress up, have more toys.*

Me: *Also true, I said, so you are freer...*

Child: *Not really... we can't go around on our own, we always have to ask permission... and also the toys, like in the park, are either broken or become boring to play with... and then again adults tell us so many nos...*

Me: *Do you agree? I asked to the class.*

Children: *(randomly), yes... in a way or another it's not easy to be a child.*

The weekend arrived and then the new week. I thought and rethought about what had happened in the last couple of weeks, with the grandparents, the children's questions, the plans. I wanted to have an interesting experience for the children. But that was the thing, not for the children, I had to remember to do it with the children. I had to balance the spontaneity of the children and their interests, but I also hat to create a space that could give an educational possibility.

I walked into the classroom with my camera. From then on it would be theirs during the day, so they could document their world. In this, I also asked their parents and grandparents for help, they could document their lives outside of school. In short, the project was to be a documentation of their childhood, from their point of view, that of the children. To understand what attracted them, to understand their disappointments, their fears, their anger, their moments of happiness and interest. Over the next few weeks, we did various activities, such as going around the town taking pictures of their places, but also their grandparents' places, seeing the differences between before and after. Understanding the history of our town, imagining how it was before our grandparents. Understanding how a town works, how to improve it for both children and grandparents. And why not, for parents as well.

A few weeks later, we created a small book for each of them with the photos we took, the drawings we made, the thoughts we had. What this experience taught me was listening, it was difficult, there were so many voices to listen to and they all deserved the same attention. It was also an experience that allowed me to put into perspective my work as an educator, my eventual being a father, but also my childhood.

Walking and w/o/a/ndering: making sense of the story

Since I was a teenager the act of walking has been a fundamental part of my life. I usually walk at least ten kilometers per day. A part of this thesis has been developed during my walks, I recorded paragraphs, discussed with friends and acquaintances about my work, re-elaborated ideas. When I walk, I see the world differently. A bit before the beginning of this doctoral path, I became a father for the first time, then I have been at home some months with a burn out, then I got my second child. I can say it has been a journey that I walked with my body and my mind. In these years the act of walking has been relevant. It helped me on several levels. However, as I showed in this work, many other educators and philosophers have walked, have w/o/a/ndered.

We walk and talk, this is life. Through walking we meet others, we experience, we get to know the world and ourselves, "walking is a profoundly social activity".[385] Walking is not just going from point A to point B, it is also going through C, D, E and F... it is a continuous discovery. This is also the sense of the last story that I displayed at the beginning of this last chapter. What we did *with* the children was an approach based on w/o/a/ndering. We tried to open up possibilities of inquiry, for example through the encounter with the grandparents, through photography, or through our wandering outside the school. We didn't have a clear path to follow, in a way I remember a sense of messiness in those weeks. We didn't have a clear plan, we were open to the unknown, we didn't want to force something. In this sense we, as educators, didn't plan to go from point A to point B. What was important was how the children picked up the fragments of life they saw, and found along the way. This is another characteristic that strikes me in children, the collecting of things, material or immaterial. A characteristic that we adults often lose. I try to keep this flame alive in me, through photography, journaling, a practice that helps me relate the outside and the inside. I would call it, thinking of Zambrano, an existentialist practice.

However, there is a passage that Ingold and Vergunst emphasise, namely how children under the age of seven are often treated as baggage when they are out and about with adults.[386] As an educator and as a father, I have noticed this. In my own way, I have always intended to give children time for urban exploration within a gentle time. For example, by planning outdoor activities where the act of discovery was more important than reaching a predetermined place. Both my children around the age of two left the stroller to walk alongside us, of course it meant taking another time, knowing that the distances and speed of the walks required a certain awareness. This awareness, however, allowed me to perceive the world through their perspective and prompted various inquiries. For instance, during our class exploration of the surroundings beyond the school, I was struck by the children's questions regarding the absence of spaces not only for themselves but also for their grandparents and parents, and their concerns about the disappearing nature. Reflecting on a photo I had at home depicting the old city surrounded by fields and woods, now vanished, I underscored this ecological sensitivity evident in their discussions. Their discourse often intertwined with imaginary realms inhabited by fairies, trolls, elves, and other magical beings. They expressed how without nature, without woods and fields, the realms of their imaginations diminished – a loss of imaginative places taken away.

Like Ward, also Ingold and Vergunst emphasise the importance of re-thinking city streets as classes:

> taking outdoors an axiom fundamental to the constitution of the classroom as an indoor learning environment, namely, that knowledge is to be pieced together through the work of head and hands, from information obtained at different locations, rather than grown along the paths children take as they make their ways on foot, from place to place, through the world about which they learn.[387]

We can say that walking means knowing.[388] As I displayed in this dissertation the practice of walking, of w/o/a/ndering, is present in all the authors presented. Maria Zambrano was in exile for decades, she travelled from Europe to Latin America, her philosophy is an existentialist philosophy, born out of her exile. Walter Kohan, in addition to travelling the world, recently embarked on a journey that took him in Freire's footsteps through Brazil, and many times his educational approach is based on walking in the places where he travels to. Paulo Freire lived part of his life in exile, travelling the world, and when in Brazil he always wandered to meet others. Colin Ward walked along the streets of his town to discover the relationship between the city and childhood. Joseph Jacotot, Simon Rodriguez, Janusz Korczak, they too w/o/a/ndered, in their lives. Of course, it is not only a physical walking but also a mental, emotional walking. As an educator I have always enjoy visiting other realities, going to other schools, other countries, meeting on social media with other educators. A way of comparison to learn new things, to reflect on my practice and try to improve myself. Moreover, walking is what Masschelein defines as a poor pedagogy, a pedagogy poor in material aids, but rich in experience.[389] A pedagogy that demands just a w/o/a/ndering.

However, I would also like to address an observation made by Ingold and Vergunst.[390] At one point they describe the relationship between walking and storytelling in an indigenous culture. What strikes me is how storytelling is used for exactly what it is, which is to tell stories. There is no didactic purpose, as Western educators are in the habit of conveying. But it is from the action produced from these stories that a moment of knowledge is generated. It means that once one embodies these stories, w/o/a/ndering and knowledge arise. So we walk and talk as in a continuous weave, in this weave we can find a moment of education and transformation. This happened in our w/o/a/n-dering with the children and the grandparents. Children told stories, their stories, immersed in an imaginary place, grandparents told stories about their past, and sometimes a playtime arose when their stories enhanced children's tales, for example confirming that once upon a time there was a magical wood, or here behind the school, trolls stopped to have a picnic. This is also a moment that I can read in twofold, on one side a sense of anarchism, where children and grandparents firstly build a relationship based on equality, and secondly create a sense of community. Moreover, children and grandparents helped each other, listened to each other, w/o/a/ndered together. On the other side there was an existentialist approach. Questions about life arose, a sense of belonging too.

Ingold, telling of the Indigenous culture Akhoe Hai//om, states "their task in life is not to occupy the world but to inhabit it".[391] This thought is the same one I try to recreate in my educational practice, and which I found as a common thread in the philosophers and educators proposed in this thesis. As an educator, I try to create the conditions in which children, and we educators as well, can reach this horizon. A condition where we do not occupy the world but inhabit it together. This means respecting the other and respecting the world itself.

I want to emphasise one last aspect of this walking practice. Kohan proposes the understanding of the verb *err* through the Latin meaning of the verb *errare*, which has two meanings, one is that of travelling, wandering, the other is that of making mistakes, erring.[392] In this understanding, in educational practice we do not only wander, we also make mistakes, but it is precisely from mistakes that we can improve our educational practice. Malatesta, argued that there is freedom even in error since no one can judge with certainty who is wrong and who is right, who is closest to the truth and which way leads best to the greatest good for all. Freedom is the only way to get, through experience, to the true and the best, there is no freedom if there is no freedom of error. Freire argues that "error and mistakes imply the adventure of the spirit. Such adventure does not take place where there is no space for freedom".[393]

In each of the experiences I had as an educator I looked back at my mistakes and tried to do better. I tried to wait for the unfolding of the situation and tiptoed into the relationship with children in proposing an educational path, not knowing where this suggestion would lead. I did many mistakes as an educator, and I continue to do them. But if at the beginning I was terrified and I saw myself as a failure, now I am aware that it happens, and I feel free to do mistakes because I know that I can do better. When I walk home, to my workplace, or just aimlessly, I have the possibility to reflect on my mistakes, on my possibilities, which can be a seed for a better educational practice. A practice that, like us human beings, is in the making or becoming.

I will address one last thing. I said that the children had a book at the end. In doing the project, I already knew that I had to give some artifacts at the end, to prove the worthiness of the educational proposal. So, I thought that a journal could have been a nice memory and a sound recognition of our work. This journal that the children had, was always with them at school and at home. They could draw, put pictures, photos, write something (or ask to write something), stick leaves or flowers, in short it was a binder for their ideas, emotions, doubts, joys, sadness, memories. In this binder, in retrospect, I can grasp their idea of w/o/a/ndering.

A pedagogy towards places of imagination

In the introduction I wrote that the purpose of this dissertation was to address, to understand, to think about the concept and practice of w/o/a/ndering and anarchism and to develop them within and through the practice of storytelling, and to think critically to the role of the educator in order to embody this creative transformative educational process. I still believe that an autoethnographic approach is a valid tool to understand our educational practice. Through stories, and experiences, we can understand, we can imagine another way of making education (make, intended as *hacer*, like we have seen through Kohan). This doesn't mean to copy uncritically other practices, but to understand, to imagine, why, how, what happens in a given practice. Even if not every author in this dissertation had a first-hand involvement with children or within early childhood education, some suggestions or some intuitions suggested can be used to remodel an educational approach.

One example is the work of Luigina Mortari and her reframing of Maria Zambrano's philosophy. Mortari reflections on the human conditions could help to better comprehend our role as educators. Mortari and Zambrano idea to be open to the uncertainty, to the other, is important, as the idea to wonder, to question ourselves in order to create a significant relationship with the other. To learn to see the world differently, even with imaginations, to foster creativity. Their existentialist philosophies give us another layer to understand human experience, and the essence of life.

Mortari urges us to recognize the significance of lived experiences in comprehending existence and shaping individual life journeys. Consequently, the educator's role extends to cultivating an educational environment conducive to nurturing children's curiosity, inquiry, and engagement with their own experiences. This is also what Kohan encourages us to do.[394]

In this sense, I understood the *a-methodical method* proposed by Mortari, and I renamed it *w/o/a/ndering*, since as an educator I try to be a w/o/a/n-derer together with the children. Through our wander, that could be done through an outdoor exploration, through playtime, through storytelling, we embody freedom, exploration and self-discovery, in our own terms.

Through her poetical philosophy, Zambrano indirectly suggests a concept that I could call "the poetics of childhood", where the imaginative nature of the experience of the child is at the center of the educational practice. It is important to foster activities like storytelling to enhance childrens' and adults' imagination. In this I consider again the act of wandering, of walking, that could be also understood as a creative act.

What about Colin Ward and anarchism? Within and outside the academia, anarchism has always been taken with skepticism, sometimes even misunderstood. Of course it is not perfect, like every human enterprise, but it can give us some interesting insights. It was not easy to portray it, because of its broad theoretical spectrum and it was impossible to squeeze it in a chapter, so I made a choice, looking mainly at the work of Colin Ward, who has done important reflections on childhood.

In my w/o/a/ndering, Ward gave me an important tool, the concept of *daily anarchism*. Ward understanding is interesting, it doesn't force any big revolution, which are often impossible to realize. Instead, he invites us to think *small*, a step-by-step process towards change. A practice that it is possible to follow daily in every educational environment if the educator decides and is willing to get involved. It's not easy, it means to challenge the order, the structure that exists in a place. A structure that it is not just as an external structure, i.e. the society, but a structure that is inside us, that we have built overtime. However, it is possible to foster Ward's daily anarchism for example during storytelling, playtime, philosophical inquiry and other daily activities, as educators we can decide where and how to engage with such practice. I proposed storytelling and playtime since they are the most common activities that children do in preschool or outside, for example in a playground.

Ward's perspective suggests that playgrounds can become oppressive if they stifle children's creativity and self-expression. This notion prompted a reconsideration of the design of indoor school spaces, aiming to collaborate with children in organizing them to facilitate freer and more imaginative play. Additionally, it led me to reflect on my approach to interact with children, whether in a hierarchical, top-down manner or in a more horizontal one. I found resonance with Ward's anarchism, which offers a pragmatic philosophical and political outlook. Many of Ward's ideas are echoed in various educational contexts, and his firsthand exploration of children's lives in the city places him not just as a theorist but as a practitioner of anarchism.

Paulo Freire has been another important author in this quest. Freire contribution to the field of education has been, and still is, very important. Sometimes it's hard to leave out something when one meets such an important theoretician and practitioner. I have decided so to gather all his important concepts, like banking education, problem-posing, dialogue, praxis but also others that sometimes are less known, like ethic. Moreover, in the chapter about Freire, two books have been mostly displayed, *Pedagogia da Autonomia*, his last work and his first work *Pedagogia do Oprimido*. I have decided to use these two books to see the beginning and the end of Freire's work (anyway chronologically).

Furthermore, Kohan has not only connected different fragments of this thesis, he has helped me connect the outside world with the inside world, that is to say: me. Kohan has given me a unique understanding within philosophy of education, and his writing has encouraged mine. When writing and educating I follow his idea, that is wandering to live, I try to think of life as a travelling school.[395] I have learned from him, but still try to make this kind of connection, to open my gaze towards new perspectives, to be curious. His understanding of childhood was something worth mentioning. He doesn't idealize childhood. If we idealize childhood, we can't really tune to it. While if we take childhood for what it is, a time in our life, an important one, but important like every human being's state, we could respect it as it deserves.

Finally, storytelling has been understood in two ways. From one side as a space where we could, as educators, foster a moment of equality, creativity, daily anarchism, and existentialism. Storytelling could be seen in many activities, like playtime, philosophical inquiry, when we w/o/a/nder or when there are more "structured" activities such as pedagogical documentation, or as Pacini-Ketchabaw called it: pedagogical narration. On the other side storytelling is embedded in the dissertation itself, in one way through my personal account as an educator, in another way through other authors accounts. Without mentioning my attempt to write in a more narrative form.

At the beginning, and for a long time, I had entitled this thesis *Homo Narrans*, because of the importance that storytelling has in the life of the human being. However, the more the dissertation took shape, the more I felt the need to change the title, therefore the title: *W/o/a/ndering towards Places of Imagination*. What is this place? What do I mean? I mean a place where we can imagine an alternative, a different way of relating to others. The choice of the title came about by rethinking precisely what the different authors who contribute to my research path have in common. In reality there are at least two things they have in common; one is precisely the possibility they see in change, in the becoming that is proper to human beings. In the words of Freire: hope, imagining other possibilities, as the world is not predetermined. The other thing they have in common is the radical humanism that transpires from their work, the trust in the human being, but also a criticism of society, of its sometimes-oppressive structure.

Here then, as an educator, I see education as a place of imagination, where we can imagine and create new relationships, where we can, in our small everydayness, propose a small change in the circumstances around us. The everyday can also be understood as a moment of play, storytelling, community of inquiry, w/o/a/ndering. All these moments are places of imagination. Without sounding presumptuous, I would also like to think of this thesis as a place of imagination, as I have felt and understood the several books I have read over the years. Books that have given me a way to think and rethink not only about my educational practice, but also about my way of being in the world, of not occupying it but inhabiting it.[396]

This dissertation has been a w/o/a/ndering for me, through authors, through my memories, through stories. It has been an important journey where I questioned myself over and over, I looked back to better understand where I'm going. It has been a journey that has helped me to embody a philosophical pedagogy that I would like to bring back firsthand as an educator in the early childhood context.

It is not easy to think about what to do next. In any case, not thinking about unsent letters, my intention is certainly to continue the exploration of creative writing in academia, to deepen my knowledge of autoethnography, not only related to the field of ECE, but also to social issues. Furthermore, I would like to continue to develop anarchism in the field of education and intertwine it with existentialism and to keep working in the philosophy with children and community of inquiry.

Notes

[385] Ingold, Tim and Vergunst, Lee (ed.). *Ways of Walking.* (Aldershot: Ashgate publishing, 2008), p.1.
[386] Ingold and Vergunst 2008.
[387] Ingold and Vergunst 2008, p.5.
[388] Masschelein, Jan. E-ducating the Gaze: the Idea of a Poor Pedagogy, *Ethics and Education*, 5:1, 43–53, (2010). DOI: 10.1080/17449641003590621
[389] Masschelein 2010.
[390] Ingold and Vergunst 2008.
[391] Ingold, Tim. *Lines: A Brief History.* (London: Routledge, 2007), p.81–84.
[392] Kohan, Walter. *Paulo Freire: a Philosophical Biography.* (London: Bloomsbury, 2021).
[393] Freire, Paulo. *Pedagogy of the Heart.* (New York: Continuum, 2000), p.89.
[394] Kohan, Walter. *Viajar para Vivir: Ensayar. La Vida como Escuela de Viaje.* (Buenos Aires: Mino y Davila, 2015).
[395] Kohan 2015.
[396] Ingold 2007.

Life is not a problem to be solved, but a reality to be experienced.
Søren Kierkegaard

References

Archibald, Jo-ann. *Indigenous Storywork.* Vancouver: UBC press, 2008.

Arkel, Dario. *Ascoltare la Luce.* Genova: Ati Editore, 2009.

Armitage, Marc. Playwork the Anarchist Wing of Sociology. In *Education, Childhood and Anarchism. Talking Colin Ward.* Catherine Burke and Ken Jones (ed.), 113–123. New York: Routledge, 2014.

Berkman, Aleksandr. *What is Anarchism?* Oakland: AK press, 2003.

Bingham, Charles and Biesta, Gert. *Jacques Rancière: Education, Truth, Emancipation.* London: Continuum publisher, 2010.

Biesta, Gert. *Good Education in an Age of Measurement: Ethics, Politics, Democracy.* Routledge: New York, 2015.

Biesta, Gert. *The Rediscovery of Teaching.* Routledge: New York, 2017.

Biffi, Elisabetta. Narrazione e Pratiche Educative: fra Infanzia e Adolescenza. In *Educare è Narrare.* Demetrio, Duccio (ed). 73–113. Milano: Mimesis Edizioni, 2012.

Castiglioni, Luigi. *Dizionario della Lingua Latina.* Milano: Loescher, 2019.

Bochner, Art. It's about time: Narrative and the Divided Self. *Qualitative Inquire, 3,* 1997, p.418–438.

Boyd, Bryan. *On the Origin of Stories.* Cambridge: Harvard University Press, 2009.

Boyd, Brian and Carroll, Joseph and Gottschall, Jonathan (ed.). *Evolution, Literature, and Film: a Reader.* New York: Columbia University Press, 2010.

Brandao, Carlos Rodriguez. Paulo Freire-a edução, a Cultura e a Universidade: Memòria de uma História de Cinquenta anos atrás. *Revista festim, natal* (1) 2, 2015. p. 157–172

Breitbart, Myrna Marguilles. Inciting Desire, Ignoring Bounderies and Making Space. In *Education, Childhood and Anarchism. Talking Colin Ward.* Cathcrine Burke and Ken Jones (ed.), 175–185. New York: Routledge, 2014

Bruner, Jerome. *La Ricerca del Significato: per una Psicologia Culturale.* Torino: Bollati Boringhieri, 1992.

Bruner, Jerome. *Making Stories.* Harvard: Harvard University Press, 2003.

Burke, Catherine, & Jones, Ken. *Education, Childhood and Anarchism.* New York: Routledge, 2014.

Caputo, Annalisa, Philosophia Ludens for Children: a Proposal to Play and to Think. In: *Thinking, Childhood, and Time.* Walter Omar Kohan and Barbara Weber (ed.), 105–116. London: Lexington Books, 2020.

Carroll, Lewis. *Alice in Wonderland.* Independently Published, 2021.

Chomsky, Noam. *Miseducation.* New York: Rowan Littlefield, 2000.

Chomsky, Noam. *On Anarchism.* New York: The new press, 2013.

Codello, Francesco. *La Buona Educazione*. Milano: Franco Angeli, 2005. Cometa, Michele. *Perché le Storie ci Aiutano a Vivere*. Milano: Raffaele Cortina editore, 2017.

Confalonieri, Emanuela and Scaratti, Giuseppe. *Storie di Crescita: Approccio Narrativo e Costruzione del sé in Adolescenza*. Unicopli: Milano, 2000.

Crowther, Kitty. *Storie della Notte*. Milano: Topipittori, 2008.

Davies, Bronwyn, & Gannon, Susanne. *Doing Collective Biography*. London: Open University Press, 2006.

DeLeon, Abraham P. How Do I Begin To Tell a Story that Has Not Been Told? Anarchism, Autoethnography, and the Middle Ground, *Equity & Excellence in Education*, 2010, 43:4, 398–413, DOI: 10.1080/10665684.2010.512828

Demetrio, Duccio. *Educare è Narrare*. Milano: Mimesis Edizioni, 2012.

Demetrio, Duccio. *Raccontarsi, l'Autobiografia come Cura di sé*. Milano: Cortina Editore, 1996.

Demetrio, Duccio. *L'Educazione non è Finita: Idee per Difenderla*. Milano: Cortina Editore, 2009.

Denzin, Norman K. *Interpretive, Autoethnography*. London: Sage, 2014.

Denzin, Norman K. *The Qualitative Manifesto. A Call to Arms*. New York: Routledge, 2019.

Dutton, Dennis. The Uses of Fiction. In *Evolution, Literature, and Film : a Reader*. Boyd, Brian and Carroll, Joseph and Gottschall, Jonathan (ed.) 184–196. New York: Columbia University Press, 2010.

Ellis, Carolyn & al. *Autoethnography. Understanding Qualitative Research*. Oxford: Oxford University press, 2015.

Eriksson, Christine. *A Preschool that Brings Children into Public Space*. Stockholm: Stockholm University, 2020.

Freire, Paulo. *We Make the Road by Walking*. Philadelphia: Temple University Press, 1990.

Freire, Paulo and Macedo, Donaldo P. *Literacy: Reading the Word [and] the World*. Routledge & Kegan Paul: London, 1987.

Freire, Paulo. *Letters to Cristina*. New York: Routledge, 1996.

Freire, Paulo. *Pedagogy of the Heart*. New York: Continuum, 2000.

Freire, Paulo. *Pedagogy of Oppressed*. New York: Continuum, 2000.

Freire, Paulo. *Pedagogia degli Oppressi*. Torino: Gruppo Abele, 2013.

Freire, Paulo. *Pedagogy of Hope: Reliving the Pedagogy of the Oppressed*. London: Bloomsbury, 2014.

Freire, Paulo. *Pedagogia della Speranza*. Torino: Gruppo Abele, 2014b.

Freire, Paulo. *Pedagogia dell'Autonomia*. Torino: Gruppo Abele, 2014c.

Freire, Paulo. *Pedagogia do Oprimido*. Porto: Edições Afrontamento, 2018.

Freire, Paulo. *Pedagogia da Autonomia*. Sao Paulo: Paz & Terra, 2019.

Goodall, H.L. *Writing the New Ethnography*. Oxford: Altamira Press, 2000.

Goodall, H.L. *Writing Qualitative Inquiry. Self, Stories and Academic Life*. New York: Routledge, 2019.

Goodman, Paul. *Compulsory Miseducation*. London: Penguin Books, 1971.

Goodman, Paul. *Growing up Absurd*. New York: NYRB, 2012.

Gottschall, Jonathan. *The Storytelling Animal: how Stories Make us Human*. New York: Mariner Books, 2013.

Graeber, David. *Fragments of an Anarchist Anthropology*. Chicago: Prickly Paradigm, 2004.

Graeber, David & Wengrow, David. *The Dawn of Everything. A New History of Humanity*. Penguin books: London, 2021.

Greene, Maxine. *Releasing the Imagination: Essays on Education, the Arts, and Social Change*. Jossey-Bass Publishers: San Francisco, 2000.

Guerin, Daniel. *Anarchism: from Theory to Practice*. New York: Monthly Review Press, 1970.

Haynes, Joanna. *Children as Philosophers*. New York: Routledge, 2008.

Haynes, Joanna and Murris, Karin. *Picturebooks, Pedagogy and Philosophy*. New York: Routledge, 2012.

Hart, Roger. Children, Self-Governance, and Citizenship. In *Education, Childhood and Anarchism. Talking Colin Ward*. Catherine Burke and Ken Jones (ed.), 123–138. Ney York: Routledge, 2014.

Haworth, Robert. *Anarchist Pedagogies, Collective Actions, Theories, and Critical Reflections on Education*. Oakland: PM press, 2012.

Haworth, Robert H. *Anarchist Education and the Modern School*. Oakland: PM press, 2019.

Henderson, Elizabeth. *Autoethnography in Early Childhood Education and Care, Narrating the Heart of Practice*. Routledge: New York: Routledge, 2018.

Herzen, Alexander. *From the Other Shore and the Russian People and Socialism*. Oxford: Oxford University press, 1979.

Huizinga, Johan. *Homo Ludens*, Kettering: Angelico Press, 2016.

Hållander, Marie. *Det Omöjliga Vittnandet*. Eskaton: Malmö: Eskaton, 2017.

Ibanez, Tomas. *Anarchia in Movimento*. Milano: Eleuthèra edizioni, 2014.

Illich, Ivan. *Nella Vigna del Testo, Per una Etologia della Lettura*. Milano: Cortina, 1994.

Ingold, Tim. *Lines: A brief History*. London: Routledge, 2007.

Ingold, Tim and Vergunst, Lee (ed.). *Ways of Walking*. Aldershot: Ashgate Publishing, 2008.

Ingold, Tim. *The Life of Lines*. Routledge: New York, 2015.

Ingold, Tim. *Anthropology and/as Education*. New York: Routledge, 2018.

Kelchtermans, Geert and Ballet, Katrjin. The Micropolitics of Teacher Induction: A Narrative-Biographical Study on Teacher Socialization. *Teaching and Teacher Education*, 18, 2002, 105–120.

Kohan, Walter. *Infanzia e Filosofia*. Perugia: Morlacchi, 2006.

Kohan, Walter and Waksman, Vera. *Fare Filosofia con i Bambini*. Napoli: Liguori Editore, 2013.

Kohan, Walter. *Il Maestro Inventore*. Roma: Aracne Editrice, 2014.

Kohan, Walter. *Philosophy and Childhood*. New York: Palgrave, 2014b.

Kohan, Walter. *The Inventive Schoolmaster*. Rotterdam: Sense Publisher, 2015.

Kohan, Walter. *Childhood, Education and Philosophy*. New York: Routledge, 2015.

Kohan, Walter. *Viajar Para Vivir: Ensayar, la Vida Como Escuela de Viaje*. Buenos Aires: Mino y Davila, 2015.

Kohan, Walter. *El Maestro Inventor. Simón Rodríguez*. Buenos Aires: Mino y Davila, 2018.

Kohan, Walter. Paulo Freire and the Childhood of a Philosophical and Educational Life in *Thinking, Childhood and Time*. Walter Omar Kohan and Barbara Weber (ed.), 131–143. London: Lexington Books, 2020.

Kohan, Walter. *Paulo Freire, a Philosophical Biography*. London: Bloomsbury, 2021.

Korczak, Janusz. *The Child's Right to Respect*. Washington: University Press of America, 1992.

Korczak, Janusz. *Il Diario dal Ghetto*. Lumi editrice: Milano, 1997.

Korczak, Janusz. *Il Diritto del Bambino al Rispetto*. Luni editrice: Milano, 2004.

Korczak, Janusz. *Come Amare il Bambino*. Lumi editrice: Milano, 2013.

Korczak, Janusz. *How to Love a Child and Other Selected Works. Vol 1–2*. Elstree: Vallentine Publisher, 2018.

Lake, Robert. *A Curriculum of Imagination in an era of Standardization: an Imaginative Dialogue*. Information Age Publishing: Charlotte, 2013.

Lester, Stuart. Play as protest. Clandestine Moments of Disturbance and Hope. In *Education, Childhood and Anarchism. Talking Colin Ward*. Catherine Burke and Ken Jones (ed.), 198–208. New York: Routledge, 2014.

Lewis, Tyson. *The Aesthetic of Education*. London: Bloomsbury, 2012.

Lodi, Mario. *Incominciare dal Bambino*. Milano: BUR, 2022.

Lorenzoni, Franco. *I Bambini Pensano Grande*. Palermo: Sellerio, 2014.

Lorenzoni, Franco. *I Bambini ci Guardano*. Palermo: Sellerio, 2019.

Lorenzoni, Franco. *Educare Controvento*. Palermo: Sellerio, 2023.

Malaguzzi, Loris. *Loris Malaguzzi and the Schools of Reggio Emilia*. (edited by Cagliari, P., Castagnetti, M., et alt.). New York: Routledge, 2016.

Malatesta, Errico. *Errico Malatesta: his Life and Ideas*. London: Freedom Press, 1993.

Marshall, Peter. *Demanding the Impossible, a History of Anarchism*. Oakland: PM press, 2010.

Masini, Pier Carlo. Prefazione in *A come Anarchia o come Apua. Un Anarchico a Carrara. Ugo Mazzucchelli*. Rosaria Bertolucci. Carrara: Quaderni della FIAP, 1988.

Masschelein, Jan and Simons, Maarten. *The Learning Society from the Perspective of Governability*. Blackwell: Oxford, 2006.

Masschelein, Jan. E-ducating the Gaze: the Idea of a Poor Pedagogy. Routledge. *Ethics and Education* Vol. 5, No. 1, March 2010, 43–53. DOI: 10.1080/17449641003590621

Masschelein, Jan and Simons, Maarten. *Rancière, Public Education and the Taming of Democracy*. Blackwell: Oxford, 2011.

Masschelein, Jan and Simons, Maarten. *In Defense of School*. Leuven: Education, Culture and Society Publishers, 2013.

Matthews, Gareth B. *Philosophy and the Young Child*. Massachusetts: Harvard UP, 1980.

Matthews, Gareth B. *Dialogues with Children*. Massachusetts: Harvard UP, 1984.

Matthews, Gareth B. *The Philosophy of Childhood*. Massachusetts: Harvard UP, 1994.

Mattia, Luisa. *A Scuola di Narrazione. Come e Perché Scrivere con i Bambini*. Casale Monferrato: Edizioni Sonda, 2011.

May, Todd. Is Post-Structuralist Political Theory Anarchist? In *Post-anarchism: a reader*. Duane Rousselle and Süreyyya Evren. 41–45. London: Pluto press, 2011.

McLaughlin, Paul. *Anarchism and Authority, a Philosophical Introduction to Classical Anarchism.* New York: Routledge, 2007.

McCarthy, Cormac. *La Strada.* Torino: Einaudi, 2006.

Melanzini, Carla. *Insegnare al Principe di Danimarca.* Palermo: Sellerio, 2023.

Milne, A.A. *Winnie the Pooh.* London: Methuen, 1949.

Mollenhauer, Klaus. *Forgotten Connections.* New York: Routledge, 2016.

Mortari, Luigina. *Un Metodo a-Metodico, la Pratica della Ricerca in Maria Zambrano.* Napoli: Liguori, 2006.

Mortari, Luigina. *Cultura della Ricerca e Pedagogia.* Roma: Carocci, 2007.

Mortari, Luigina. *A Scuola di Libertà.* Milano: Raffaello Cortina Editore, 2008.

Mortari, Luigina. *Maria Zambrano.* Milano: Feltrinelli, 2019.

Moore, Robin. Design for Urban Play as an Anarchist parable. In *Education, Childhood and Anarchism. Talking Colin Ward.* Catherine Burke and Ken Jones (ed.), 139–156. Ney York: Routledge, 2014.

Mueller, Justin. Anarchism, the State and the Role of Education. In *Anarchist Pedagogies: Collective Actions, Theories, and Critical Reflections on Education.* Haworth, Robert H. (ed.), 14–31. Oakland: PM press, 2012.

Nicholson, Simon. The Theory of Loose Parts. *Studies in Design Education Craft & Technology* 4 (2), pp.5–14, 1972. http://jil.lboro.ac.uk/ojs/index.php/SDEC/article/view/1204/1171

Niles, John. *Homo Narrans, The Poetics and Anthropology of Oral Literature.* Philadelphia: UoP Press, 1999.

Ortega y Gasset, Josè. *Historia Como Sistema y Otros Ensayos de Filosofia.* Alianza editorial, 2003.

Ortega y Gasset, Josè. *Meditations on Quixote.* New York: The Norton library, 1963.

Pacini-Ketchabaw, Veronica et al. *Journeys, Reconceptualizing ECP through Pedagogical Narration.* Toronto: UTP, 2015.

Pacini-Ketchabaw, Veronica and Taylor, Affrica. *Unsettling the Colonial Places and Spaces of Early Childhood Education.* New York: Routledge, 2015b.

Pacini-Ketchabaw, Veronica et al. *Encounters with Materials in Early Childhood Education.* New York: Routledge, 2017.

Pritchard, Michael, "Philosophy for Children", *The Stanford Encyclopedia of Philosophy,* (Summer 2022 Edition), Edward N. Zalta (ed.), URL=<https://plato.stanford.edu/archives/sum2022/entries/children/>

Rancière, Jacques. *The Ignorant Schoolmaster.* Stanford: Stanford University Press, 2007.

Rancière, Jacques. *Il Maestro Ignorante.* Milano: Mimesis Edizioni, 2008.

Ranke, Kurt. *Problems of Categories in Folk Prose.* (1967), accessed through https://it.scribd.com/document/465720749/Homo-narrans-Ranke

Rinaldi, Carlina. *In Dialogo con Reggio Emilia, Ascoltare, Ricercare e Apprendere.* Reggio Emilia: Reggio Children, 2009.

Ritzer, George. *The McDonalidisation of Society.* Thousand Oaks: Pine Forge press, 1993.

Schempp, Paul. *The Micro-politics of Teacher Induction,* American Educational Research Journal, 30 (3), 1993, pp. 447–472.

Scott-Brown, Sophie. *Colin Ward and the Art of Everyday Anarchy.* London: Routledge, 2023.

Sendak, Maurice. *Nel Paese dei Mostri Selvaggi.* Milano: Adelphi, 2018.

Simons, Maarten and Masschelein, Jan. From Schools to Learning Environments: The Dark Side of Being Exceptional. *Journal of Philosophy of Education of Great Britain*, Vol. 42, No. 3–4, 2008

Smorti, Andrea. *Il Pensiero Narrativo: Costruzione di Storie e Sviluppo della Conoscenza Sociale.* Giunti Stampa: Firenze, 1994.

Solnit, Rebecca. *Wanderlust: A History of Walking.* New York: Penguin Books, 2001.

Suissa, Judith. *Anarchism and Education: a Philosophical Perspective.* Oakland: PM press, 2010.

Sævi Tone, and Norm Friesen, Norm (2010) 'Reviving forgotten connections in North American teacher education: Klaus Mollenhauer and the pedagogical relation', *Journal of Curriculum Studies*, 42, pp. 123–147.

Tan, Shaun. *The Lost Thing.* London: Hodder Children's Books, 2010.

Tan, Shaun. *The Arrival.* London: Hodder Children's Books, 2014.

Trasatti, Filippo. *Lessico Minimo di Pedagogia Libertaria.* Milano: Eleuthèra Editrice, 2014.

Tyson, Lewis. *The Aesthetics of Education.* New York: Continuum, 2012.

VV.AA. I Cento Linguaggi dei Bambini. Bergamo: Edizioni Junior, 2010.

VV.AA. *Noi Scriviamo Forme che Sembrano Libri.* Reggio Children: Reggio Emilia, 2008a.

VV.AA. *I Giardini Sono…* Reggio Children: Reggio Emilia, 2008b.

Walford , Geoffrey. Finding the limits: Autoethnography and Being an Oxford University Proctor. 403–417. *Qualitative Research* , 4 (3). 2004.

Ward, Colin. *The Child in the City.* London: Architectural Press, 1978.

Ward, Colin. *Influences.* London: Greenbooks, 1991.

Ward, Colin. *Tallking School.* Freedom Press: London, 1995.

Ward, Colin. *Anarchism a Very Short Introduction.* Oxford: Oxford UP, 2004.

Ward, Colin. *Talking Anarchy.* Oakland: PM press, 2014.

Ward, Colin. *Anarchy in Action.* Oakland: PM press, 2018.

Wilbert, Chris and White, Damian F. *Autonomy, solidarity, possibility, the Colin Ward Reader.* Oakland: AK press, 2011.

Worth, Sara. Storytelling and Narrative Knowing: an Examination of the Epistemic Benefits of Well-told Stories. *The Journal of Aesthetic Education*, 42, p.42–56. 2008.

Zambrano, Maria. *I Beati.* Feltrinelli: Milano, 1992.

Zambrano, Maria. *Verso un Sapere dell'Anima.* Milano: Cortina, 1996.

Zambrano, Maria. *Filosofia e Poesia.* Bologna: Pendragon, 1998.

Zambrano, Maria. *Delirio e Destino.* Milano: Cortina, 2000.

Zambrano, Maria. *Note di un Metodo.* Napoli: Filema, 2003.

Zambrano, Maria. *Chiari del Bosco.* Milano: Bruno Mondadori, 2004.

Zambrano, Maria. *Sogni e Tempo.* Bologna: Pendragon, 2004b.

Södertörn Doctoral Dissertations

1. Jolanta Aidukaite, *The Emergence of the Post-Socialist Welfare State: The case of the Baltic States: Estonia, Latvia and Lithuania*, 2004

2. Xavier Fraudet, *Politique étrangère française en mer Baltique (1871–1914): de l'exclusion à l'affirmation*, 2005

3. Piotr Wawrzeniuk, *Confessional Civilising in Ukraine: The Bishop Iosyf Shumliansky and the Introduction of Reforms in the Diocese of Lviv 1668–1708*, 2005

4. Andrej Kotljarchuk, *In the Shadows of Poland and Russia: The Grand Duchy of Lithuania and Sweden in the European Crisis of the mid-17th Century*, 2006

5. Håkan Blomqvist, *Nation, ras och civilisation i svensk arbetarrörelse före nazismen*, 2006

6. Karin S Lindelöf, *Om vi nu ska bli som Europa: Könsskapande och normalitet bland unga kvinnor i transitionens Polen*, 2006

7. Andrew Stickley. *On Interpersonal Violence in Russia in the Present and the Past: A Sociological Study*, 2006

8. Arne Ek, *Att konstruera en uppslutning kring den enda vägen: Om folkrörelsers modernisering i skuggan av det Östeuropeiska systemskiftet*, 2006

9. Agnes Ers, *I mänsklighetens namn: En etnologisk studie av ett svenskt biståndsprojekt i Rumänien*, 2006

10. Johnny Rodin, *Rethinking Russian Federalism: The Politics of Intergovernmental Relations and Federal Reforms at the Turn of the Millennium*, 2006

11. Kristian Petrov, *Tillbaka till framtiden: Modernitet, postmodernitet och generationsidentitet i Gorbačevs glasnost' och perestrojka*, 2006

12. Sophie Söderholm Werkö, *Patient patients? Achieving Patient Empowerment through Active Participation, Increased Knowledge and Organisation*, 2008

13. Peter Bötker, *Leviatan i arkipelagen: Staten, förvaltningen och samhället. Fallet Estland*, 2007

14. Matilda Dahl, *States under scrutiny: International organizations, transformation and the construction of progress*, 2007

15. Margrethe B. Søvik, *Support, resistance and pragmatism: An examination of motivation in language policy in Kharkiv, Ukraine*, 2007

16. Yulia Gradskova, *Soviet People with female Bodies: Performing beauty and maternity in Soviet Russia in the mid 1930–1960s*, 2007

17. Renata Ingbrant, *From Her Point of View: Woman's Anti-World in the Poetry of Anna Świrszczyńska*, 2007

18. Johan Eellend, *Cultivating the Rural Citizen: Modernity, Agrarianism and Citizenship in Late Tsarist Estonia*, 2007

19. Petra Garberding, *Musik och politik i skuggan av nazismen: Kurt Atterberg och de svensk-tyska musikrelationerna*, 2007

20. Aleksei Semenenko, *Hamlet the Sign: Russian Translations of Hamlet and Literary Canon Formation*, 2007

21. Vytautas Petronis, *Constructing Lithuania: Ethnic Mapping in the Tsarist Russia, ca. 1800–1914*, 2007

22. Akvile Motiejunaite, *Female employment, gender roles, and attitudes: The Baltic countries in a broader context*, 2008

23. Tove Lindén, *Explaining Civil Society Core Activism in Post-Soviet Latvia*, 2008

24. Pelle Åberg, *Translating Popular Education: Civil Society Cooperation between Sweden and Estonia*, 2008

25. Anders Nordström, *The Interactive Dynamics of Regulation: Exploring the Council of Europe's monitoring of Ukraine*, 2008

26. Fredrik Doeser, *In Search of Security After the Collapse of the Soviet Union: Foreign Policy Change in Denmark, Finland and Sweden, 1988–1993*, 2008

27. Zhanna Kravchenko. *Family (versus) Policy: Combining Work and Care in Russia and Sweden*, 2008

28. Rein Jüriado, *Learning within and between public-private partnerships*, 2008

29. Elin Boalt, *Ecology and evolution of tolerance in two cruciferous species*, 2008

30. Lars Forsberg, *Genetic Aspects of Sexual Selection and Mate Choice in Salmonids*, 2008

31. Eglė Rindzevičiūtė, *Constructing Soviet Cultural Policy: Cybernetics and Governance in Lithuania after World War II*, 2008

32. Joakim Philipson, *The Purpose of Evolution: 'struggle for existence' in the Russian-Jewish press 1860–1900*, 2008

33. Sofie Bedford, *Islamic activism in Azerbaijan: Repression and mobilization in a post-Soviet context*, 2009

34. Tommy Larsson Segerlind, *Team Entrepreneurship: A process analysis of the venture team and the venture team roles in relation to the innovation process*, 2009

35. Jenny Svensson, *The Regulation of Rule-Following: Imitation and Soft Regulation in the European Union*, 2009

36. Stefan Hallgren, *Brain Aromatase in the guppy, Poecilia reticulate: Distribution, control and role in behavior*, 2009

37. Karin Ellencrona, *Functional characterization of interactions between the flavivirus NS5 protein and PDZ proteins of the mammalian host*, 2009

38. Makiko Kanematsu, *Saga och verklighet: Barnboksproduktion i det postsovjetiska Lettland*, 2009

39. Daniel Lindvall, *The Limits of the European Vision in Bosnia and Herzegovina: An Analysis of the Police Reform Negotiations*, 2009

40. Charlotta Hillerdal, *People in Between – Ethnicity and Material Identity: A New Approach to Deconstructed Concepts*, 2009

41. Jonna Bornemark, *Kunskapens gräns – gränsens vetande*, 2009

42. Adolphine G. Kateka, *Co-Management Challenges in the Lake Victoria Fisheries: A Context Approach*, 2010

43. René León Rosales, *Vid framtidens hitersta gräns: Om pojkar och elevpositioner i en multietnisk skola*, 2010

44. Simon Larsson, *Intelligensaristokrater och arkivmartyrer: Normerna för vetenskaplig skicklighet i svensk historieforskning 1900–1945*, 2010

45. Håkan Lättman, *Studies on spatial and temporal distributions of epiphytic lichens*, 2010

46. Alia Jaensson, *Pheromonal mediated behaviour and endocrine response in salmonids: The impact of cypermethrin, copper, and glyphosate*, 2010

47. Michael Wigerius, *Roles of mammalian Scribble in polarity signaling, virus offense and cell-fate determination*, 2010

48. Anna Hedtjärn Wester, *Män i kostym: Prinsar, konstnärer och tegelbärare vid sekelskiftet 1900*, 2010

49. Magnus Linnarsson, *Postgång på växlande villkor: Det svenska postväsendets organisation under stormaktstiden*, 2010

50. Barbara Kunz, *Kind words, cruise missiles and everything in between: A neoclassical realist study of the use of power resources in U.S. policies towards Poland, Ukraine and Belarus 1989–2008*, 2010

51. Anders Bartonek, *Philosophie im Konjunktiv: Nichtidentität als Ort der Möglichkeit des Utopischen in der negativen Dialektik Theodor W. Adornos*, 2010

52. Carl Cederberg, *Resaying the Human: Levinas Beyond Humanism and Antihumanism*, 2010

53. Johanna Ringarp, *Professionens problematik: Lärarkårens kommunalisering och välfärdsstatens förvandling*, 2011

54. Sofi Gerber, *Öst är Väst men Väst är bäst: Östtysk identitetsformering i det förenade Tyskland*, 2011

55. Susanna Sjödin Lindenskoug, *Manlighetens bortre gräns: Tidelagsrättegångar i Livland åren 1685–1709*, 2011

56. Dominika Polanska, *The emergence of enclaves of wealth and poverty: A sociological study of residential differentiation in post-communist Poland*, 2011

57. Christina Douglas, *Kärlek per korrespondens: Två förlovade par under andra hälften av 1800-talet*, 2011

58. Fred Saunders, *The Politics of People – Not just Mangroves and Monkeys: A study of the theory and practice of community-based management of natural resources in Zanzibar*, 2011

59. Anna Rosengren, *Åldrandet och språket: En språkhistorisk analys av hög ålder och åldrande i Sverige cirka 1875–1975*, 2011

60. Emelie Lilliefeldt, *European Party Politics and Gender: Configuring Gender-Balanced Parliamentary Presence*, 2011

61. Ola Svenonius, *Sensitising Urban Transport Security: Surveillance and Policing in Berlin, Stockholm, and Warsaw*, 2011

62. Andreas Johansson, *Dissenting Democrats: Nation and Democracy in the Republic of Moldova*, 2011

63. Wessam Melik, *Molecular characterization of the Tick-borne encephalitis virus: Environments and replication*, 2012

64. Steffen Werther, *SS-Vision und Grenzland-Realität: Vom Umgang dänischer und „volksdeutscher" Nationalsozialisten in Sønderjylland mit der „großgermanischen" Ideologie der SS*, 2012

65. Peter Jakobsson, *Öppenhetsindustrin*, 2012

66. Kristin Ilves, *Seaward Landward: Investigations on the archaeological source value of the landing site category in the Baltic Sea region*, 2012

67. Anne Kaun, *Civic Experiences and Public Connection: Media and Young People in Estonia*, 2012

68. Anna Tessmann, *On the Good Faith: A Fourfold Discursive Construction of Zoroastripanism in Contemporary Russia*, 2012

69. Jonas Lindström, *Drömmen om den nya staden: Stadsförnyelse i det postsovjetisk Riga*, 2012

70. Maria Wolrath Söderberg, *Topos som meningsskapare: Retorikens topiska perspektiv på tänkande och lärande genom argumentation*, 2012

71. Linus Andersson, *Alternativ television: Former av kritik i konstnärlig TV-produktion*, 2012

72. Håkan Lättman, *Studies on spatial and temporal distributions of epiphytic lichens*, 2012

73. Fredrik Stiernstedt, Mediearbete i mediehuset: Produktion i förändring på MTG-radio, 2013

74. Jessica Moberg, *Piety, Intimacy and Mobility: A Case Study of Charismatic Christianity in Present-day Stockholm*, 2013

75. Elisabeth Hemby, *Historiemåleri och bilder av vardag: Tatjana Nazarenkos konstnärskap i 1970-talets Sovjet*, 2013

76. Tanya Jukkala, *Suicide in Russia: A macro-sociological study*, 2013

77. Maria Nyman, *Resandets gränser: Svenska resenärers skildringar av Ryssland under 1700-talet*, 2013

78. Beate Feldmann Eellend, *Visionära planer och vardagliga praktiker: Postmilitära landskap i Östersjöområdet*, 2013

79. Emma Lind, *Genetic response to pollution in sticklebacks: Natural selection in the wild*, 2013

80. Anne Ross Solberg, *The Mahdi wears Armani: An analysis of the Harun Yahya enterprise*, 2013

81. Nikolay Zakharov, *Attaining Whiteness: A Sociological Study of Race and Racialization in Russia*, 2013

82. Anna Kharkina, *From Kinship to Global Brand: The Discourse on Culture in Nordic Cooperation after World War II*, 2013

83. Florence Fröhlig, *A painful legacy of World War II: Nazi forced enlistment: Alsatian/Mosellan Prisoners of war and the Soviet Prison Camp of Tambov*, 2013

84. Oskar Henriksson, *Genetic connectivity of fish in the Western Indian Ocean*, 2013

85. Hans Geir Aasmundsen, *Pentecostalism, Globalisation and Society in Contemporary Argentina*, 2013

86. Anna McWilliams, *An Archaeology of the Iron Curtain: Material and Metaphor*, 2013

87. Anna Danielsson, *On the power of informal economies and the informal economies of power: Rethinking informality, resilience and violence in Kosovo*, 2014

88. Carina Guyard, *Kommunikationsarbete på distans*, 2014

89. Sofia Norling, *Mot "väst": Om vetenskap, politik och transformation i Polen 1989–2011*, 2014

90. Markus Huss, *Motståndets akustik: Språk och (o)ljud hos Peter Weiss 1946–1960*, 2014

91. Ann-Christin Randahl, *Strategiska skribenter: Skrivprocesser i fysik och svenska*, 2014

92. Péter Balogh, *Perpetual borders: German-Polish cross-border contacts in the Szczecin area*, 2014

93. Erika Lundell, *Förkroppsligad fiktion och fiktionaliserade kroppar: Levande rollspel i Östersjöregionen*, 2014

94. Henriette Cederlöf, *Alien Places in Late Soviet Science Fiction: The "Unexpected Encounters" of Arkady and Boris Strugatsky as Novels and Films*, 2014

95. Niklas Eriksson, *Urbanism Under Sail: An archaeology of fluit ships in early modern everyday life*, 2014

96. Signe Opermann, *Generational Use of News Media in Estonia: Media Access, Spatial Orientations and Discursive Characteristics of the News Media*, 2014

97. Liudmila Voronova, *Gendering in political journalism: A comparative study of Russia and Sweden*, 2014

98. Ekaterina Kalinina, *Mediated Post-Soviet Nostalgia*, 2014

99. Anders E. B. Blomqvist, *Economic Natonalizing in the Ethnic Borderlands of Hungary and Romania: Inclusion, Exclusion and Annihilation in Szatmár/Satu-Mare, 1867–1944*, 2014

100. Ann-Judith Rabenschlag, *Völkerfreundschaft nach Bedarf: Ausländische Arbeitskräfte in der Wahrnehmung von Staat und Bevölkerung der DDR*, 2014

101. Yuliya Yurchuck, *Ukrainian Nationalists and the Ukrainian Insurgent Army in Post-Soviet Ukraine*, 2014

102. Hanna Sofia Rehnberg, *Organisationer berättar: Narrativitet som resurs i strategisk kommunikation*, 2014

103. Jaakko Turunen, *Semiotics of Politics: Dialogicality of Parliamentary Talk*, 2015

104. Iveta Jurkane-Hobein, *I Imagine You Here Now: Relationship Maintenance Strategies in Long-Distance Intimate Relationships*, 2015

105. Katharina Wesolowski, *Maybe baby? Reproductive behaviour, fertility intentions, and family policies in post-communist countries, with a special focus on Ukraine*, 2015

106. Ann af Burén, *Living Simultaneity: On religion among semi-secular Swedes*, 2015

107. Larissa Mickwitz, *En reformerad lärare: Konstruktionen av en professionell och betygssättande lärare i skolpolitik och skolpraktik*, 2015

108. Daniel Wojahn, *Språkaktivism: Diskussioner om feministiska språkförändringar i Sverige från 1960-talet till 2015*, 2015

109. Hélène Edberg, *Kreativt skrivande för kritiskt tänkande: En fallstudie av studenters arbete med kritisk metareflektion*, 2015

110. Kristina Volkova, *Fishy Behavior: Persistent effects of early-life exposure to 17α-ethinylestradiol*, 2015

111. Björn Sjöstrand, *Att tänka det tekniska: En studie i Derridas teknikfilosofi*, 2015

112. Håkan Forsberg, *Kampen om eleverna: Gymnasiefältet och skolmarknadens framväxt i Stockholm, 1987–2011*, 2015

113. Johan Stake, *Essays on quality evaluation and bidding behavior in public procurement auctions*, 2015

114. Martin Gunnarson, *Please Be Patient: A Cultural Phenomenological Study of Haemodialysis and Kidney Transplantation Care*, 2016

115. Nasim Reyhanian Caspillo, *Studies of alterations in behavior and fertility in ethinyl estradiol-exposed zebrafish and search for related biomarkers*, 2016

116. Pernilla Andersson, *The Responsible Business Person: Studies of Business Education for Sustainability*, 2016

117. Kim Silow Kallenberg, *Gränsland: Svensk ungdomsvård mellan vård och straff*, 2016

118. Sari Vuorenpää, *Literacitet genom interaction*, 2016

119. Francesco Zavatti, *Writing History in a Propaganda Institute: Political Power and Network Dynamics in Communist Romania*, 2016

120. Cecilia Annell, *Begärets politiska potential: Feministiska motståndsstrategier i Elin Wägners 'Pennskaftet', Gabriele Reuters 'Aus guter Familie', Hilma Angered-Strandbergs 'Lydia Vik' och Grete Meisel-Hess 'Die Intellektuellen'*, 2016

121. Marco Nase, *Academics and Politics: Northern European Area Studies at Greifswald University, 1917–1992*, 2016

122. Jenni Rinne, *Searching for Authentic Living Through Native Faith – The Maausk movement in Estonia*, 2016

123. Petra Werner, *Ett medialt museum: Lärandets estetik i svensk television 1956–1969*, 2016

124. Ramona Rat, *Un-common Sociality: Thinking sociality with Levinas*, 2016

125. Petter Thureborn, *Microbial ecosystem functions along the steep oxygen gradient of the Landsort Deep, Baltic Sea*, 2016

126. Kajsa-Stina Benulic, *A Beef with Meat Media and audience framings of environmentally unsustainable production and consumption*, 2016

127. Naveed Asghar, *Ticks and Tick-borne Encephalitis Virus – From nature to infection*, 2016

128. Linn Rabe, *Participation and legitimacy: Actor involvement for nature conservation*, 2017

129. Maryam Adjam, *Minnesspår: Hågkomstens rum och rörelse i skuggan av en flykt*, 2017

130. Kim West, *The Exhibitionary Complex: Exhibition, Apparatus and Media from Kulturhuset to the Centre Pompidou, 1963–1977*, 2017

131. Ekaterina Tarasova, *Anti-nuclear Movements in Discursive and Political Contexts: Between expert voices and local protests*, 2017

132. Sanja Obrenović Johansson, *Från kombifeminism till rörelse: Kvinnlig serbisk organisering i förändring*, 2017

133. Michał Salamonik, *In Their Majesties' Service: The Career of Francesco De Gratta (1613–1676) as a Royal Servant and Trader in Gdańsk*, 2017

134. Jenny Ingridsdotter, *The Promises of the Free World: Postsocialist Experience in Argentina and the Making of Migrants, Race, and Coloniality*, 2017

135. Julia Malitska, *Negotiating Imperial Rule: Colonists and Marriage in the Nineteenth century Black Sea Steppe*, 2017

136. Natalya Yakusheva, *Parks, Policies and People: Nature Conservation Governance in Post-Socialist EU Countries*, 2017

137. Martin Kellner, *Selective Serotonin Re-uptake Inhibitors in the Environment: Effects of Citalopram on Fish Behaviour*, 2017

138. Krystof Kasprzak, *Vara – Framträdande – Värld: Fenomenets negativitet hos Martin Heidegger, Jan Patočka och Eugen Fink*, 2017

139. Alberto Frigo, *Life-stowing from a Digital Media Perspective: Past, Present and Future*, 2017

140. Maarja Saar, *The Answers You Seek Will Never Be Found at Home: Reflexivity, biographical narratives and lifestyle migration among highly-skilled Estonians*, 2017

141. Anh Mai, *Organizing for Efficiency: Essay on merger policies, independence of authorities, and technology diffusion*, 2017

142. Gustav Strandberg, *Politikens omskakning: Negativitet, samexistens och frihet i Jan Patočkas tänkande*, 2017

143. Lovisa Andén, *Litteratur och erfarenhet i Merleau-Pontys läsning av Proust, Valéry och Stendhal*, 2017

144. Fredrik Bertilsson, *Frihetstida policyskapande: Uppfostringskommissionen och de akademiska konstitutionerna 1738–1766*, 2017

145. Börjeson, Natasja, *Toxic Textiles – towards responsibility in complex supply chains*, 2017

146. Julia Velkova, *Media Technologies in the Making – User-Driven Software and Infrastructures for computer Graphics Production*, 2017

147. Karin Jonsson, *Fångna i begreppen? Revolution, tid och politik i svensk socialistisk press 1917–1924*, 2017

148. Josefine Larsson, *Genetic Aspects of Environmental Disturbances in Marine Ecosystems – Studies of the Blue Mussel in the Baltic Sea*, 2017

149. Roman Horbyk, *Mediated Europes – Discourse and Power in Ukraine, Russia and Poland during Euromaidan*, 2017

150. Nadezda Petrusenko, *Creating the Revolutionary Heroines: The Case of Female Terrorists of the PSR (Russia, Beginning of the 20th Century)*, 2017

151. Rahel Kuflu, *Bröder emellan: Identitetsformering i det koloniserade Eritrea*, 2018

152. Karin Edberg, *Energilandskap i förändring: Inramningar av kontroversiella lokaliseringar på norra Gotland*, 2018

153. Rebecka Thor, *Beyond the Witness: Holocaust Representation and the Testimony of Images – Three films by Yael Hersonski, Harun Farocki, and Eyal Sivan*, 2018

154. Maria Lönn, *Bruten vithet: Om den ryska femininitetens sinnliga och temporala villkor*, 2018

155. Tove Porseryd, *Endocrine Disruption in Fish: Effects of 17α-ethinylestradiol exposure on non-reproductive behavior, fertility and brain and testis transcriptome*, 2018

156. Marcel Mangold, *Securing the working democracy: Inventive arrangements to guarantee circulation and the emergence of democracy policy*, 2018

157. Matilda Tudor, *Desire Lines: Towards a Queer Digital Media Phenomenology*, 2018

158. Martin Andersson, *Migration i 1600-talets Sverige: Älvsborgs lösen 1613–1618*, 2018

159. Johanna Pettersson, *What's in a Line? Making Sovereignty through Border Policy*, 2018

160. Irina Seits, *Architectures of Life-Building in the Twentieth Century: Russia, Germany, Sweden*, 2018

161. Alexander Stagnell, *The Ambassador's Letter: On the Less Than Nothing of Diplomacy*, 2019

162. Mari Zetterqvist Blokhuis, *Interaction Between Rider, Horse and Equestrian Trainer – A Challenging Puzzle*, 2019

163. Robin Samuelsson, *Play, Culture and Learning: Studies of Second-Language and Conceptual Development in Swedish Preschools*, 2019

164. Ralph Tafon, *Analyzing the "Dark Side" of Marine Spatial Planning – A study of domination, empowerment and freedom (or power in, of and on planning) through theories of discourse and power*, 2019

165. Ingela Visuri, *Varieties of Supernatural Experience: The case of high-functioning autism*, 2019

166. Mathilde Rehnlund, *Getting the transport right – for what? What transport policy can tell us about the construction of sustainability*, 2019

167. Oscar Törnqvist, *Röster från ingenmansland: En identitetsarkeologi i ett maritimt mellanrum*, 2019

168. Elise Remling, *Adaptation, now? Exploring the Politics of Climate Adaptation through Post-structuralist Discourse Theory*, 2019

169. Eva Karlberg, *Organizing the Voice of Women: A study of the Polish and Swedish women's movements' adaptation to international structures*, 2019

170. Maria Pröckl, *Tyngd, sväng och empatisk timing – förskollärares kroppsliga kunskaper*, 2020

171. Adrià Alcoverro, *The University and the Demand for Knowledge-based Growth The hegemonic struggle for the future of Higher Education Institutions in Finland and Estonia*, 2020

172. Ingrid Forsler, *Enabling Media: Infrastructures, imaginaries and cultural techniques in Swedish and Estonian visual arts education*, 2020

173. Johan Sehlberg, *Of Affliction: The Experience of Thought in Gilles Deleuze by way of Marcel Proust*, 2020

174. Renat Bekkin, *People of reliable loyalty…: Muftiates and the State in Modern Russia*, 2020

175. Olena Podolian, *The Challenge of 'Stateness' in Estonia and Ukraine: The international dimension a quarter of a century into independence*, 2020

176. Patrick Seniuk, *Encountering Depression In-Depth: An existential-phenomenological approach to selfhood, depression, and psychiatric practice*, 2020

177. Vasileios Petrogiannis, *European Mobility and Spatial Belongings: Greek and Latvian migrants in Sweden*, 2020

178. Lena Norbäck Ivarsson, *Tracing environmental change and human impact as recorded in sediments from coastal areas of the northwestern Baltic Proper*, 2020

179. Sara Persson, *Corporate Hegemony through Sustainability – A study of sustainability standards and CSR practices as tools to demobilise community resistance in the Albanian oil industry*, 2020

180. Juliana Porsani, *Livelihood Implications of Large-Scale Land Concessions in Mozambique: A case of family farmers' endurance*, 2020

181. Anders Backlund, *Isolating the Radical Right – Coalition Formation and Policy Adaptation in Sweden*, 2020

182. Nina Carlsson, *One Nation, One Language? National minority and Indigenous recognition in the politics of immigrant integration*, 2021

183. Erik Gråd, *Nudges, Prosocial Preferences & Behavior: Essays in Behavioral Economics*, 2021

184. Anna Enström, *Sinnesstämning, skratt och hypokondri: Om estetisk erfarenhet i Kants tredje Kritik*, 2021

185. Michelle Rydback, *Healthcare Service Marketing in Medical Tourism – An Emerging Market Study*, 2021

186. Fredrik Jahnke, *Toleransens altare och undvikandets hänsynsfullhet – Religion och meningsskapande bland svenska grundskoleelever*, 2021

187. Benny Berggren Newton, *Business Basics – A Grounded Theory for Managing Ethical Behavior in Sales Organizations*, 2021

188. Gabriel Itkes-Sznap, *Nollpunkten. Precisionens betydelse hos Witold Gombrowicz, Inger Christensen och Herta Müller*, 2021

189. Oscar Svanelid Medina, *Att forma tillvaron: Konstruktivism som konstnärligt yrkesarbete hos Geraldo de Barros, Lygia Pape och Lygia Clark*, 2021

190. Anna-Karin Selberg, *Politics and Truth: Heidegger, Arendt and The Modern Political Lie*, 2021

191. Camilla Larsson, *Framträdanden: Performativitetsteoretiska tolkningar av Tadeusz Kantors konstnärskap*, 2021

192. Raili Uibo, *"And I don't know who we really are to each other": Queers doing close relationships in Estonia*, 2021

193. Ignė Stalmokaitė, *New Tides in Shipping: Studying incumbent firms in maritime energy transitions*, 2021

194. Mani Shutzberg, *Tricks of the Medical Trade: Cunning in the Age of Bureaucratic Austerity*, 2021

195. Patrik Höglund, *Skeppssamhället: Rang, roller och status på örlogsskepp under 1600-talet*, 2021

196. Philipp Seuferling, *Media and the refugee camp: The historical making of space, time, and politics in the modern refugee regime*, 2021

197. Johan Sandén, *Närbyråkrater och digitaliseringar: Hur lärares arbete formas av tids-strukturer*, 2021

198. Ulrika Nemeth, *Det kritiska uppdraget: Diskurser och praktiker i gymnasieskolans svenskundervisning*, 2021

199. Helena Löfgren, *Det legitima ägandet: Politiska konstruktioner av allmännyttans privatisering i Stockholms stad 1990–2015*, 2021

200. Vasileios Kitsos, *Urban policies for a contemporary periphery: Insights from eastern Russia*, 2022

201. Jenny Gustafsson, *Drömmen om en gränslös fred: Världsmedborgarrörelsens reaktopi, 1949–1968*, 2022

202. Oscar von Seth, *Outsiders and Others: Queer Friendships in Novels by Hermann Hesse*, 2022

203. Kristin Halverson, *Tools of the Trade: Medical Devices and Practice in Sweden and Denmark, 1855–1897*, 2022

204. Henrik Ohlsson, *Facing Nature: Cultivating Experience in the Nature Connection Movement*, 2022

205. Mirey Gorgis, *Allt är våld: En undersökning av det moderna våldsbegreppet*, 2022

206. Mats Dahllöv, *Det absoluta och det gemensamma: Benjamin Höijers konstfilosofi*, 2022

207. Anton Poikolainen Rosén, *Noticing Nature: Exploring More Than Human-Centred Design in Urban Farming*, 2022

208. Sophie Landwehr Sydow, *Makers, Materials and Machines: Understanding Experience and Situated Embodied Practice at the Makerspace*, 2022

209. Simon Magnusson, *Boosting young citizens' deontic status: Interactional allocation of rights-to-decide in participatory democracy meetings*, 2022

210. Marie Jonsson, *Vad vilja vegetarianerna? En undersökning av den svenska vegetarismen 1900–1935*, 2022

211. Birgitta Ekblom, *Härskarhyllning och påverkan: Panegyriken kring tronskiftet 1697 i det svenska Östersjöväldet*, 2022

212. Joanna Mellquist, *Policy Professionals in Civil Society Organizations: Struggling for Influence*, 2022

213. David Birksjö, *Innovative Security Business – Innovation, Standardization and ndustry Dynamics in the Swedish Security Sector, 1992–2012*, 2023

214. Roman Privalov, *After space utopia: Post-Soviet Russia and futures in space*, 2023

215. Martin Johansson, *De nordiska lekarna: Grannlandsrelationen i pressen under olympiska vinterspel*, 2023

216. Anna Bark Persson, *Steel as the Answer? Viking Bodies, Power, and Masculinity in Anglophone Fantasy Literature 2006–2016*, 2023

217. Josefin Hägglund, *Demokratins stridslinjer: Carl Lindhagen och politikens omvandling, 1896–1923*, 2023

218. Lovisa Olsson, *I vinst och förlust: Köpmäns nätverk i 1500-talets Östersjöstäder*, 2023

219. Kateryna Zorya, *The Government Used to Hide the Truth, But Now We Can Speak: Contemporary Esotericism in Ukraine 1986–2014*, 2023

220. Tony Blomqvist Mickelsson, *A Nordic sport social work in the context of refugee reception*, 2023

221. Ola Luthman, *Searching for sustainable aquaculture governance: A focus on ambitions and experience*, 2023

222. Emma Kihl, *Äventyrliga utföranden: En läsning av Agneta Enckells dikter med Isabelle Stengers kosmopolitik*, 2023

223. Cagla Demirel, *Analyzing Competitive Victimhood: Narratives of recognition and non-recognition in the pursuit of reconciliation*, 2023

224. Joel Odebrant, *Spår, kropp, tid: En undersökning av den måleriska gestens materialitet 1952–1965*, 2024

225. Xiaoying Li, *Energy Efficiency in Buildings in the Baltic States and the Nordic Countries*, 2024

226. Thérese Janzén, *Ticks – Ecology, New Hazards, and Relevance for Public Health*, 2024

227. Paul Sherfey, *Cultivating Responsible Citizenship: Collective Gardens at the Periphery of Neoliberal Urban Norms*, 2024

228. Kirill Polkov, *Queering Images of Russia in Sweden: Discursive hegemony and counter-hegemonic articulations 1991–2019*, 2024

229. Karl Katz Lydén, *Critique and the Care of the Self: The Economy of Truth and Government in Michel Foucault's Late Work*, 2024

230. Matteo Enrico Cattaneo, *Woandering towards places of imagination: Reflections through anarchism on the role of educators in early childhood education*, 2024

9 789189 504844